T0082568

SAGA of an

Angry Young Black Man

authorHOUSE®

AuthorHouse™
1663 Liberty Drive
Bloomington, IN 47403
www.authorhouse.com
Phone: 1 (800) 839-8640

© *2017 Harvey Williams Jr. All rights reserved.*

No part of this book may be reproduced, stored in a retrieval system, or transmitted by any means without the written permission of the author.

Published by AuthorHouse 04/05/2017

ISBN: 978-1-5246-8677-2 (sc)
ISBN: 978-1-5246-8676-5 (e)

Library of Congress Control Number: 2017905218

Print information available on the last page.

Any people depicted in stock imagery provided by Thinkstock are models, and such images are being used for illustrative purposes only. Certain stock imagery © Thinkstock.

This book is printed on acid-free paper.

Because of the dynamic nature of the Internet, any web addresses or links contained in this book may have changed since publication and may no longer be valid. The views expressed in this work are solely those of the author and do not necessarily reflect the views of the publisher, and the publisher hereby disclaims any responsibility for them.

CONTENTS

1

THE SCHOOL OF LIFE

When the clocks were set ahead one hour in 1970, most people viewed it as Daylight Saving Time but for me, it meant hour closer to me being on my own. The day of graduation was rapidly approaching and I was one frighten young man. I started taking a serious look at my life and wondering what my future would be like...What I would become. Up to that point, high school had been one big playground for me and instead of getting an education, I was more concerned about getting girls and attention. For the past three years, I had been living in fantasyland but now reality was starting to set in. Prior to DST, whenever I thought about what life would be like after high school, I just figured I would cross that bridge when I got to it. With only two months of school left, I saw that bridge and it was not as far away as it had been. Suddenly, the days started to seem like hours; and the weeks like days; and the months like weeks. Before I could put together my future plans, the day of graduation, June 2, 1970, was upon me.

When my name was called during the graduation ceremony and I was handed my diploma, it was as though I had been handed the key to the gate of life and commanded to go. I watched as several classmates ran, leaping, and tossing their hats into the air but for me there was nothing to celebrate. Although I had walked and talked like a man during the last years of school, I knew that I was not ready to face life on my own. I was terrified! The day after graduation, I started work at a trailer (mobile home) plant in Douglas, Ga. I was somewhat excited about going to work because I wanted to buy a car but for the most part, I wished I were still in school but there was no turning back the hands of time. Even if I wanted to go to college, I feared not being able to past the entry exam; therefore, higher learning was not an option…or so I thought at the time. During the 30-minute drive to the trailer plant, I wondered what my job duties would be. I was 5 ft. 11 inches tall and weighed approximately 140 pounds; therefore, I had anticipated doing light work, something that did not require heavy lifting. My uncle, who had recommended me for the job, had been employed at the plant for several years and I was confident that "his" work record would pave the way for me to get an easy job…but I was in for a rude awakening. I was about to be introduced to the school of life.

When we arrived at the job site, which was too fast for me, my uncle took me to the office and left. I remember thinking, "Where's he going?" I thought he would tell the boss good things about me and he (the boss) would give me a light, smooth, easy job. That was the first sign that I had entered into the real world and that I was truly on my own. After filling out an application (and other necessary forms), I was escorted to the department where I would be working and introduced to the foreman. The foreman was approximately my size but a bit older and I noticed he was panting and sweating…and it was early. The fact that he was the foreman, and he was sweating caused me to wonder what my job duties would be. Above the sound of buzzing saws, nail guns firing, clamping staplers, and pounding hammers, the foreman shouted out my job description to me, as he appeared somewhat impatient and eager to get back to work.

After a few minutes of listening to what appeared to be foreign language, I was given a tool belt filled with unfamiliar tools and introduced to the guy I would be working with. Needless to say, this guy was also panting and sweating…and working extremely fast. It soon became very obvious that neither the foreman, nor the guy training me were going to be holding my hand. This was not a classroom, this was life and I was not prepared. But this was by no means my first job. I had worked in the fields during the summer months when school was out since I was 6-years old. I had hoed corn, pulled weeds out of peanuts, suckled, topped and cropped tobacco and picked cotton. During the two years prior to graduation, I'd worked after school at the sawmill, which was primarily by choice. But now, I had no choice when it came to working because that's what the school of life was about…learning to secure your livelihood.

After being at the trailer plant a few hours, I knew the foreman was not going to tell or show me how to do the same thing twice. I was expected to grasp what I was told the first time because everything was on the move…even the trailers being built. I soon realized that the foreman was my boss and not my teacher. He was in charge of making make sure I did my job. My uncle was in the same building but I didn't see him anywhere. I was alone with this trainer/ stranger who was trying to show me the proper way to hold a hammer and drive a nail. I could see the frustration on his face, as if he was wondering why I'd been hired in the first place. There was no homework or books to study that would teach me how to do my job but I wanted to believe that I would "catch on" and learn like everybody else there had. However, deep down within I had my doubts, which soon turned into fear, which gradually started turning into anger.

I noticed that everyone around me was working hard, fast, and were sweating. No one was idling around like I'd done so often in the fields and at the sawmill. I saw men lifting and carrying heavy walls up steps, as they worked feverously to complete the mobile home they were assembling. I thought to myself, "How in the world can two men lift and carry all that weight?" I wouldn't have to wonder long. I can't remember all my job duties but I do remember the part that involved me carrying those heavy walls up steps and setting them down to be secured in place. I'd never worked anywhere that required me to do heavy lifting. I had loaded watermelons a few years earlier but only for a day (I was too sore to return the next day). I also remember thinking my employer knew I was not physically fit to lift and carry those heavy walls. Although both black and white men alike were lifting and carrying walls all around me, I convinced myself that I was being treated unfairly because I was black.

I ignored the fact that I had refused to get an education while in school that would have prepared me for college or trade school. I looked overlooked (dismissed) my faults and blamed others for my disposition and before the day was over, anger had completely consumed me. When the shift was over, I told my uncle on the way back home that I would not be lifting walls the next day because they were too heavy. He said he would talk with his boss to see if he would give me a lighter job but said nothing else during the rest of the drive. He was probably thinking what I mistake he'd made by recommending me for the job. Nevertheless, I fully expected him to "fix it" for me the next day since he'd been working there so long. But after he dropped me off at my mother's house, I wondered how well he would be able to fix it, as he drove away.

After toiling all day at the trailer plant, I was exhausted and aching all over…discovering muscles in my body I never knew were there. I could not believe that I had been expected to perform such strenuous labor! I knew absolutely nothing about building (or assembling) mobile homes and I certainly was in no shape to do all the required heavy lifting. Why had I been given such strenuous work? Was it because I was black and my boss was a white man? Although, I saw white men toiling alongside black men, doing the same job, I lay in bed that night trying hard to convince myself that I was experiencing racism and prejudice. It mattered little to me that the man helping me carry the heavy walls was white. It was my first mental attempt at playing the race card. Although I had a high school diploma, I did not have a high school education. I was such a terror and disruption during my final high school years that I was told (by a teacher) that if would just put my head down on the desk and not cause problems, he would pass me to the next grade. I thought it was cool at the time but did not realize it was tantamount to being kicked out of school. I was a cool fool and didn't know it.

Like school, I expected to receive special treatment in the real world, especially since I was black. The Civil Rights Movement was ending and white people, for the most part, seemed to have been trying to make up for how they (and their ancestors) had treated black people in the past. This was also during the "Black Power" movement and I expected my white employer to give me a break… simply because I was black. After all, things were changing in the south and my boss had an obligation to prove to me that he was not prejudice. I really believed at the time that being black was more important than seeking higher education or learning a trade. My forefathers had been mistreated and therefore, I felt a sense of entitlement and expected some type of restitution. I went to bed that night anticipating a change in job duties the next day…and that's exactly what I got.

I got up early the next morning, still aching from the day before, and prepared myself physically, mentally, and emotionally for work. During the 30-minute drive to the plant, I again reminded my uncle that I would quit if the employer did not give me a lighter job. It mattered not at all to me that he had recommended me for the job. The only thing that concerned me was what I wanted, which was a lighter job. I can only imagine what my uncle was thinking (probably how naïve and ungrateful I was) but he agreed to speak with the employer about reassigning me to another area. After arriving at the plant and clocking in, I went to my assigned work area. I watched my uncle go into the office. I started working hard and fast, as I had done the day before but expecting to be moved at any moment. The minutes slowly turned into an hour and still no change. I started to get angry but outwardly, I remained calm by convincing myself that my employer was busy trying to find a suitable position for me. In the meantime, I slowed my paced so that it would be obvious to everyone that I was not physically fit to perform my assigned heavy duties. Not only was I a skinny black man, to whom they were obligated to prove that they were not prejudice, but my uncle and cousin also worked there. Surely, I would be shown some degree of favoritism. Nevertheless, I had decided the night before that if not given lighter duties by the first morning break, I was quitting.

After what seemed like forever, it was time for the morning break. I was angry that my employer had not rescued me from hard labor and without saying a word to anyone, I grabbed my lunch, clocked out...and walked off the job. After walking approximately 5 miles, I was picked up by someone from Willacoochee and given a ride home. When my uncle came by the house that evening, he stated that the boss would have moved me had I not walked off the job. Whether or not this would have happened, I'll never know. However, there was one thing that was perfectly clear. I was a young black man with no education, no job skills, and no money, which made me an unemployed nobody...who wanted to be somebody but didn't really want to work. A few weeks later, I went to work in the tobacco field...but only for a day. While sliding a metal rack of tobacco out of a trailer, the rail securing the tobacco came loose and in a rage, I picked up the rail and slammed it to the ground. In the process, I slammed my left hand against the trailer, which resulted in a trip to the hospital and four stitches. Unable to work for the next few weeks, I had lots of time to think about my future. I really wanted to be back in high school but I had graduated and was now enrolled in the school of life, which was nothing like high school.

2

FORT JACKSON

I decided that since I couldn't get a decent job at home I would join the military and live off Uncle Sam. I was fully aware that the country was at war with Viet Nam and that American lives were being lost on a weekly basis. I thought if I joined the U. S. Navy I would be safe from combat and besides, I liked the uniforms. I convinced a schoolmate and friend of mine to enlist with me because I really did not want to wander out into the world alone. We talked with a recruiter and he promised that if we joined together, we could serve together. My friend and I were sent to Jacksonville, Florida where we took the entry exam. I passed the written test but unfortunately, he did not. I decided that if he could not join the Navy, then neither would I. We were best friends and had gone through high school together. I could not leave him behind.

A few weeks later, we both decided that we would enlist in the U. S. Army. I really didn't want to join the Army because nothing about that branch of service appealed to me. Not only did I hate the ill-fitting olive drab (and khaki) uniforms, I knew that the chances of me being sent to fight in Viet Nam were great. The U. S. Marines had sharp, colorful, neat-fitting uniforms but the basic training was more than I was willing to tolerate. The Air Force had nice blue uniforms and seemed rather laid back but my friend and I was told (by someone) that the entry exam was difficult; therefore, we decided we would join the Army. Feeling somewhat reluctant, I contacted an Army recruiter and we took the took the test and this time we both passed. After filling out all the necessary paperwork, we were given a date of departure and we were overflowing with joy.

On September 31, 1970, we said goodbye to our families and caught the Trailways bus to Jacksonville, Fl. where we both would be sworn into the U.S. Army, or so we thought. Once inside the processing center in Jacksonville, we went separate ways and when I saw him again I could tell something was wrong. He fought back tears as he stated, "Man, I can't go with you. They say I failed the written test." I didn't know what to say to him but I couldn't return home. I had been catching lots of heat from my Mom for not having a job, so for me it was either the Army or a life of hard, physical labor on some dead-end job. I embraced my friend, said goodbye and was sworn into the U.S. Within a few hours, I was on my way to Fort Jackson, S.C.

During the long bus ride to Ft. Jackson, I started to feel lonely as I thought about my friends back home. Not only that but I had never been so far away from home. Had I known my friend would not be able to accompany me, I would not have enlisted in the Army but there was no turning back now. I could have changed my mind before I was sworn in but everyone expected me to leave and I didn't want to return home with some lame excuse as to why I didn't follow through. I also did not want to tell them that my friend had failed the written exam. I didn't realize that adulthood would be so lonely and frightening. Like any normal person, I feared the unknown. I was quiet, as I watched and listen to the other recruits laugh and joke about everything under the sun. Some even made fun of the bus driver whenever he occasionally turned on the wipers to clear the windshield. Someone joked, "Do anybody other than the driver see the rain?" The driver only glanced into the rearview mirror as if to say, "Buddy, in just few hours you'll be singing a totally different song." The glance into the mirror did not lie.

Upon arriving at the Reception Station in Ft. Jackson, personal identity started to disappear as soon as we stepped off the bus. No one was laughing or joking now. There were men in uniforms screaming instructions so loud that you could not hear or understand them. Whenever instructed to step forward, most stepped back and when instructed to move to the left, most moved to the right. I was nervous but not really frighten. I kept calm by convincing myself that all the chaos was necessary and that it would help me to become a man. Except for having to take numerous shots and pull a two-hour watch, starting at midnight, life at the Reception Station was not that bad. I filled out forms, received uniforms, shoes, boots, underwear, etc., and instructions on how to dress. An officer also prepped us on what we would experience during basic training. He told us that his first day in boot camp was so terrifying that he was literally shaking in his boots but I told myself that it would not happen to me. After all, the drill sergeants were trained to do what they do and there was nothing for me to fear. I'd heard they were not allowed to put their hands on a recruit in a violent manner; therefore, I wasn't concerned about the men wearing the "Smokey" hats. I was only slightly concerned about the physical aspect of the training.

After two weeks at the Reception Station, we were transported to boot camp on the back of a truck. Upon arrival, we were met by drill instructors yelling, "Grab your gear and hit the ground!" When my feet touched the ground, I was (literally) shaking in my boots so badly that I could barely stand. In fact, I was shaking so badly that it took one of the kinder drill instructors to come over and calm me down. He whispered in my ear, "It's alright, Son. Just pay attention." The other drill instructors were in our face, screaming like rabid dogs and acting as if they were going to bite our nose off at any moment. I was so terrified that l could not think or comprehend anything I was commanded to do. These mad men were screaming for us to stand in attention, turn left, turn right...and a whole lot of other gibberish that amounted to foreign language. Again, the kinder sergeant came to my rescue. He instructed me to align my thumbs with the seam of my pants when standing in attention. Later that evening, we went to the mess hall but had no appetite but I was encouraged to eat...because I was going to need all the strength I get during the next six weeks. That night I was awakened at 2:00 A.M. to pull a two-hour watch, wearing full uniform, helmet and carrying a baseball bat. I thought to myself, "How stupid this is." But refusing was not an option. When my watch was over, I had approximately one hour to rest before the rigorous training day begun. That day would be the beginning of the end of my life as a potential soldier in the U. S. Army.

Around 5:00 a.m., a drill sergeant came into the dorm like a tornado, screaming obscenities and shoving recruits around. I thought to myself, "I thought they couldn't put their hands on the recruits." To whom can this poor guy complain to? The sergeant had already told us the day before that we had entered into "his" world and that he was now our mama and daddy...and that no other mama and daddy would be able to help us. I really didn't like how he made reference to "mama" but I was in his world and had to abide by his rules, whether I liked them or not. Later that morning, we marched to a field where physical basic training began. It was early October and unusually warm for that time of year. One of the exercises involved holding an M16 at arm's length while squatting. It wasn't long before my thighs started to burn from the strain, as well as my arms, so I lowered my rifle. Immediately, a drill sergeant rushed over and started calling me everything except a child of God. I raised the weapon again, kinda wishing it was loaded (for obvious reasons) but soon lowered it again. When the sergeant returned to confront me again, I just laid on my back and stared up at the sky. Although I felt and smelt his breathe on my face, I blocked out the sound so that I could not hear his words. After a minute or so, I got up and finished the exercise...as I listened to him make fun of me while the other recruits laughed.

When we returned to the dorm, one of the drill instructors yell for me to, "Git your A** Over Here, NOW!" When I did not come quick enough, he ordered me to run back to the starting point and come again, and again, and again, and again, and again...until I tripped, striking my head against a bunk bed. When I regained consciousness a few second later, I was totally unfamiliar with my surrounding. But standing over me was this big black man, dressed in an olive-green uniform and wearing a Smokey the Bear hat, yelling obscenities and ordering me to get up. After a few minutes of sheer terror, I remembered that I was in the Army…but I pretended not to know where or who I was. Not only did I know where or who I was, I knew who I was going to become and that was civilian again. I saw the accident as my ticket out of boot camp, out of the army, and a one-way ticket back home. So, I faked having amnesia and would not respond to any stimulants such as dog tags, photo id, documents, etc. After being examined for an hour or so by a physician, I was transferred to the hospital and placed on Ward 49 a.k.a. the "crazy ward."

Ward 49 was reserved for recruits suffering from mental disorders. I was by no means crazy but I was amongst people who were. I remember being in the recreation room and playing billiards with this guy who without warning, grabbed a ball and slammed it into the light over the table. There was also this Native American who had a habit of staring others down. He was muscular and weighed probably 225 pounds. At the time, I must have weighed no more than 135 lbs. but whenever he'd try to stare me down, he always lost. Although, he appeared to be macho, I saw in his eyes that he was a wimp and like myself, had ended up in the wrong place and was now trying to get back home.

As the days on Ward 49 turned into a week, I became extremely depressed and was placed in a private room where I slept most of the days away. Occasionally, I would come out to watch TV but I mostly just slept, being awaken occasionally by staff to take medication and/or to eat. I just wanted to go home and the physician wasn't telling me anything. In the meantime, I started hearing these horror stories about basic training and Viet Nam. I don't know which troubled me the most but I was determined not to experience either. The idea of crawling underneath barbed wire with live rounds whizzing over my head, and getting bloody knees did not appeal to me at all; Nor did marching 10 miles with 50 or 60 lbs. strapped to my back. Nor did running five miles before breakfast (or anytime) appeal to me; Nor did doing 100 pushups in heat, rain, sleet and snow appeal to me. I don't know how much of what I was told was true but determined that I was not going to stick around to find out.

I decided that I was not going to basic training, nor was I going to Viet Nam…even it meant during my stint on the ward. I had actually signed up for a tour in Viet Nam at the Reception Station when I arrived but now I remembered the expression on the face of the soldier processing my papers. He stopped writing and asked, "Are you sure you want to sign up for Viet Nam?" I had an uncle that had served in Viet Nam and I remembered him telling me that soldiers who went to war ranked faster than those who remained in the States. But didn't tell me at the time that he was a Supply Sergeant and therefore, never actually experienced combat. Nevertheless, when I began to hear about what was really happening in Viet Nam, I decided that I was not going.

While confined to Ward 49, I called my mother daily, pleading with her to come and visit me because I was so lonely and I was homesick. I just needed to hear a familiar voice and see a familiar face. I had heard about homesickness and thought I understood it but I had not a clue what it was like. A few weeks prior to enlisting in the Army, I had attempted to console my brother, who had left home for the first time and had gotten homesick. Now I was experiencing the same thing and needed someone to console me. Like my brother, no advice could cure my homesickness. Now that old saying, "If you ain't been there, then you don't know what it's like," had taken on a whole new meaning. To my relief, my mother finally agreed to come and visit me. As the weekend of her visit drew near, the hours seem like days and the days like weeks. But a few days before the scheduled visit, my mother informed me that they would not be coming. She said it would be best for me not see them, and then have to watch them leave. What she didn't know, but must have sensed, is that I had no intention of them returning home without me...even if it meant me going AWOL, escaping in the trunk of the car.

When I received news that they were not coming, I became extremely depressed, crying entire day and most of the night. I refused to eat or drink anything that day. Although I was being treated well, I felt as though I was a prisoner in a strange land. I started to wonder if I would ever return home again. Two or three days after learning Mom and other relatives would not be coming to visit me, I made a superficial attempt at suicide. I had become desperate to return home and was determined to get there by any means necessary...but I wanted to arrive alive. I was able to get a bottle of Aspirin and swallow 10 or 12 tablets but I timed everything so that staff would be checking on me within 10 or 15 minutes after I swallowed them. I arranged the bottle (and the remainder of the tablets) in a manner that would suggest that I had taken an overdose. It worked. I was rushed down to another room and given some concoction that caused me to vomit. After being monitored for two or three hours, I was taken back to the ward and placed on suicide watch. This was not good for me because rather than be allowed to sleep most of the day, staff was now checking on me at random, which interfered with my sleep and sleep had become my mental escape. If only I had known in high school that being on my own would be so rough, I would have taken education much more seriously.

Approximately two weeks after the "suicide attempt," a psychiatrist with ice blue piercing eyes walked into the room and stated, "Son, you want to go home, don't you?" I started to cry and said, "Yes, Sir." He then stated very calmly, "You're going home, Son." I thanked him and wanted to ask when I would be leaving but did not for fear that he might be playing some kind of trick on me. Nevertheless, I did call my mother and gave her the good news. She was happy for me but must have wondered what I would do with my life now that I was coming back home. I was told by the hospital staff that I would be leaving as soon as they could process me out, which would be approximately 14 days. I experienced a mixture of both joy and pain. I was happy to know when I was leaving but one the other hand, I became even more depressed as the hours to countdown started to seem days and the days into weeks. When asked if I wanted to apply for a Medical Discharge, I stated that I did. That was until I was informed that by doing so would delay my discharge. Needless to say, I told the gentleman to forget it. I was glad to be getting an Honorable Discharge but would have settled for a Dishonorable, or anything in between, so long as I was getting out of the Army. The reason listed for discharge on my DD214 was "Not physically fit at time of enlistment." But the truth of the matter was, I was not "mentally" or "emotionally" fit at time of enlistment.

During my final week at Fort Jackson, I did pretty much as I pleased. I was not quick to obey orders because I knew I was going home and therefore, was not concerned about being disciplined. I even snuck into town with a group of recruits (that had earned a pass) and went to a bar. I even refused to shave...up until the last two days before being officially discharged. A sergeant stopped me and asked if I had forgotten how to shave and I stated, "No Sir!" He then proceeded to tell me how ridiculous I looked and how I'd better respect the uniform I was wearing. I thought to myself, "Buddy, I've got plans for this uniform as soon as I get on the bus." The day of my departure finally arrived and while sitting in a room with other rejects waiting to be processed out, again we were asked if anyone wanted to apply for a Medical Discharge. I think one recruit raised his hand and was told to remain after everyone else was dismissed. I really wanted to apply for a Medical Discharge because I had gotten a glimpse of what the real world was like. I was not ready to be a man, working for a living. I wanted to be taken care of financially, as in getting something for doing nothing. But my desire to get back home far exceeded my desire to remain in the Army one hour more than necessary. I was given $250.00, a Grey Hound bus ticket and driven to the bus station in Columbia, South Carolina.

I was eager to return home but I wanted to return a changed person. So, while waiting for the bus to arrive, I bought a pack of Kent cigarettes. I had never smoked a cigarette before but always thought people who did were cool. No one whom I knew smoked Kent cigarettes and I wanted to smoke a brand that was different. When I took my first drag (inhaled) of the cigarette, I thought I would die from coughing, as I struggled to breathe. When a bystander asked if I was all right, I told her I had a cold but I'm sure she knew differently. I was really embarrassed...but not enough to stop trying to smoke that cigarette. Each drag got easier and smoother and after coughing through half of that first cigarette, I was able to finish without further incident. This made me feel like a man, as I envisioned myself talking to others with a cigarette hanging from the corner of my mouth. In fact, I was determined to get addicted to cigarettes. I did not want to pretend to be a smoker, I wanted the craving, the habit...the whole nine yards. I wanted to be so I could not function properly without a cigarette...because I thought smoking would be a shortcut to manhood. I wasn't concerned about staining my already neglected teeth, or having bad breath and I was too naïve at the time to be concerned about cancer.

When the bus arrived at the station, I took my army issued shirt out my pants, undid my tie, and position my hat in the opposite manner in which I had been instructed to wear it. It was a blatant display of defiance, although the Army had done nothing to me, except try to make me a man. Several people looked on me in disgust that day but I didn't care. One gentleman stated to me that if the Army knew how I was disgracing their uniform, I would be locked up. I told him what the Army didn't know wouldn't hurt them. I moved to the back of the bus and continued to smoke the ill tasting cigarettes until I had developed a style of my own. I practiced inhaling the smoke and blowing it out the side of my mouth and through my nostrils. A young fool in the making! As the bus drew nearer to Willacoochee, I began to get concerned about what people were going to say and think about me. Most would definitely know I had experienced a "nervous breakdown" and that I had been confined to Ward 49 (the crazy house) while in the Army. What they didn't know was I had faked amnesia to get out of the Army. But if I told them, then they would never respect me as a sane man. If I told them that I'd hit my head and got amnesia, they would think I was crazy for real. So, just what would I tell them? I didn't know but I would think of something.

When I arrived in Willaccochee, two of my closest friends were waiting at the bus depot in Douglas, Ga. to give me a ride home. The first thing I said to them when I stepped off the bus was, "I hear James Brown has gotten Super Bad since I been gone." This was in reference to Mr. Brown's song, "Super Bad," that I'd first heard while on Ward 49. We all had a good laugh and headed to Willacoochee so I could greet my family…for a few minutes. Afterwards, we went to "Pop's Place," a local hole in the wall juke joint, and sat under the big oak tree. I had missed my two friends so badly and I believe the feeling was mutual. I pulled out a wad of money and stated, "Uncle Sam takes care of his boys too." We sat there under the tree for hours, drinking beer, smoking cigarettes and listening to music. I was so glad to be back home.

Although I was glad to be back, it was not my intention to stay in Willaccoochee. It was a nice place to live but too small and the best jobs were at least 20 miles away. But even those jobs (chicken processing plants, trailer plants and textile mills) had very little to offer. I needed more and I knew I was not going to find it in Willaccochee; therefore, one week after being discharged from the Army, I signed up for the Jobs Corp and learned I would be going to San Marcos, Texas. In the meantime, I went to work part-time at the local sawmill. It was autumn and my Army uniform was perfect for shielding me from the cold wind that blew through the stacks of lumber. In the weeks to come, the Army coat would become filthy and tattered from making contact with the tarry lumber. I didn't understand why I was so angry with the Army but I was. Maybe it was because I had been exposed as a failure.

A week or so after returning home, I met a young lady from Florida. Although we dated, I was not interested in falling in love. I was 18-years old and I'd already had my heart broken; therefore, I wasn't about to lower my (emotional) guard again. She knew I was leaving and constantly begged me stay but her pleads fell on deaf ears. She was only sixteen and wanted to have a child together and get married. She told me I was her I was her first love but the only thing on my mind was getting out of Willacoochee. I had no idea what life would be like in Texas, but I was ready to go.

The friend that had been denied entry into the Army during the time I enlisted decided that he also wanted to go to the Job Corps. I was glad because I really didn't want to leave home alone again. I no longer feared getting homesick because someone told me that it only happens once. Not only that but I just didn't think it would happen to me again because I had taken a sincere look at my options if I did not leave and that alone would be enough to keep me from wanting to return. On December 2, 1970, my friend and I were driven to Waycross, Ga. where we boarded a bus headed for San Marcos, Texas. Ironically, I had stayed in the Army six weeks and now six weeks after being discharged I was on headed to the Job Corps. The young lady who had fallen in love accompanied my friend and I to the post office, where we were to be picked up by the recruiter, pleading with me to stay. Within, I was hurting for her because I felt her pain but I didn't show it. I just told her that I had to leave and that I would write her…but I never did; although, she wrote me several times. After two months, she stopped writing.

3

JOB CORPS

I knew very little about the Jobs Corps, other than it was a government funded program that offered free training for people aged 16 to 21, that want to learn a trade. I was assured that upon completion of the program that I would be guaranteed employ that in the field of my trade. This was exactly what I needed, since I had wasted away the latter part of my high school years doing everything except learning what was being taught. My initial plans were to train in auto upholstery so I could go to Detroit and work at the Ford Motor Company where my friend's sister had been employed for several years. In fact, he had join for the same reason.

After traveling for two days by Grey Hound, we finally arrived at Gary Jobs Corp Center in the wee hours of the morning. We were photographed and given these dull green uniforms, shoes and an Id badge that were to be worn on at all times. We were also given a set of rules to abide by, as well as a set of disciplinary actions should we break any of those rules We were introduced to the base police squad, which were made up of hardcore corpsmen who appeared eager to stomp heads with their spit-shine combat boots. They had the authority to make arrests...

by whatever means necessary. I found my new home to be somewhat like the Army I'd just left but not nearly as strict. I was told the JC center was an abandoned Air Force base. Nevertheless, there was no one yelling obscenities at you, nor were there any requirement to say "yes sir" or "No Sir." Everyone was referred to by his or her first name.

The corpsmen were a mixture of Negroes, Hispanics and a few white males. I was assigned to 3211 Blue Block where I shared a dorm room with eight other guys, four to a room with bunk beds. Blue Block was reserved for guys training to learn a trade in the automotive industry. The entire dorm consisted of five rooms that housed a total of twenty corpsmen. Everyone in my dorm room was black. I later learned that most of the corpsmen at the center had a criminal background and had been given the option of joining the Jobs Corp or being locked up; however, this did not bother me in the least bit. I had no intention of bothering anyone and I was not going to allow anyone to bother me…or my friend, with whom I shared a room. We had both a dorm manager and a dorm leader. The manager was a nice older white gentleman we called "Pops" and he was responsible for the entire Blue Block section, which consisted of at least ten dorms.

The dorm leader was a corpsman that lived in one of the dorms. He was responsible for all twenty corpsmen and the condition of their dorm rooms. He reported directly to the dorm manager. Then there was Lucas, a black guy who came around every morning at 6:00 a.m. to wake us up. Lucas was a huge burly guy but he was friendly, if you didn't give him any problems. We could hear him making his way to each of the Blue Block dorms, knocking on doors and windows, telling the guys that it was time to get up. Fifteen minutes later, he would revisit each dorm to make sure everyone was up. My dorm leader at the time was a guy from Louisiana who did not really care about the condition of the dorm, so long as it passed the weekly inspection. He seemed more interested in Red Block than he did his own. Red Block housed the base known homosexuals. Most were training to be nurses and chefs but not everyone housed in Red Block was gay.

The pay for a new corpsman was $14.22 every two weeks, which might not seem like much but it was the early 70's and the government paid all living expenses (food, shelter and clothing). Dorm leaders and base policemen received $5 more than the average corpsman. However, one could earn more pay by earning merits...but could lose pay if they received demerits or infractions. Demerits meant not only would one lose pay but be restricted to the base as well. On Wednesday, Friday and Saturday we were allowed to visit San Marcos, Austin and San Antonio. Those of us who had money, and were not restricted to base, often went to San Marcos on Wednesday since the base was located only a few miles from downtown. But on Friday and Saturday pay weeks, most of us boarded the powder blue buses and went either to Austin or San Antonio. I enjoyed both cities but San Antonio was my favorite. The trip to the cities were always fun, as I anticipated being in the big city, free as a bird to wander the streets in search of excitement. However, the trip back to the base was a totally different story. Often the guys would get drunk while in town and vomit during the trip back to the center. Needless to say, the driver did not pull over and let these guys off the bus to throw up. Imagine the smell of vomit and alcohol in the confinement of the bus, not to mention this filth flowing beneath your feet from the back of the bus during the 50-mile trip back to the center. It was absolutely horrible!

I enjoyed visiting Austin and going into the state capitol building and calling my mother at least once a month. There was not really a lot to do in Austin, except get into trouble while trying to date the local girls, which often resulted in being chased back to the bus by the local guys. One night in Austin, I met a young lady at the skating ring and she convinced me to go home with her to meet her parents. It was one of the few times that I had gotten a weekend pass, which meant I could leave the base on Friday evening and not have to return until Sunday evening. Reluctantly, I accompanied the young lady to her house on Hemlock Street, where she lived with her parents. No sooner had I entered the house and sat down, one of her sisters came home. Her father started to scold this sister for leaving the house and when she started to talk back, he grabbed her and then slammed her down on a coffee table…breaking it into pieces.

I sat there, frozen in fear, not knowing what to expect next. The father then looked at me with bloodshot eyes and shouted, "AND YOU, NIGGA, GET OUT AND DON'T EVER COME BACK!" I got up, hoping he would not strike me as I walked hastily towards the door. I knew that if he'd broken a table with his own flesh and blood, he would kill me. When I was several blocks down the streets, I heard someone calling my name and when I turned and to see who it was I realized it was the madman's daughter who had invited me to meet her parents. She apologized for all the madness and then stated that she did not want to go back home. She didn't leave me until the next day when it was time to check out of the hotel. I have no idea as to how she fared when she returned home because I never saw or spoke with saw her again.

San Antonio was approximately 50 miles from the center and it was the place to go if you really wanted to party. There was a nightclub there named The Frisky-A-Go-Go, where bikini clad females danced to the tunes of a Mexican band that played American hit songs. At the club, we would meet local girls and buy them a drink or two. If we were lucky, we would be rewarded with a kiss before having to leave and catch the bus back to the center before it departed for the base around midnight. One night at the club, the young ladies showered a few of us guys with a little more affection that usual, which meant that they appeared to actually want us to hang around awhile. When we finally discovered that all they really wanted was more drinks, it was too late for us to catch the bus back to the base. When we had spent all, the girls went home (but not before I got a kiss) and we went to the Grey Hound Bus Station and called the center, informing them that we had missed the bus. The dorm manager sent a car to get us but not before the next morning. Such behavior usually automatically resulted in loss of pay and restriction to the base but for some reason, we were never punished and I never missed the bus again.

Three months after arriving at the center, the dorm leader graduated and went back to Louisiana. I was then appointed, by the dorm manager, as the new dorm leader. It was a huge responsibility, as I had to deal with several guys in the dorm that was court ordered to be there. It was my responsibility to get them up in the morning and they were not always happy about that, especially when recovering from a hangover. The night manager, Lucas, would come into the other dorms each morning between 5:30 and 6:00 a.m., yelling for everyone to get out of bed but not our dorm. He would simply walk past my widow and give a light tap on the widow and I would tap in return to assure him that I was awake. Many of the court-ordered corpsmen were thugs but most were not. Most gave me the utmost respect and I respected them in return. I cared nothing about their criminal past, only their behavior while were under my supervision. I would inspect the dorm daily and if I found anything out of order, or dust where it should not be, I gave the guys a warning. If I found the same problem again, I gave them a write-up, which meant they would receive a demerit (reduction in pay) for a month or more.

Shortly after being appointed to dorm leader, my best friend enlisted in the Air Force. Now I was alone again in a strange land…surrounded by hundreds of strange people. I took the entry exam with him but decided that it would be in my best interest to reveal to the recruiter that I had enlisted in the Army, been discharged and given a 4-F rating. As expected, he informed me that I was not qualified to enlist into the Air Force. I was somewhat saddened because I wanted to remain with my friend but I had no problem adjusting to life without him. However, I did change my trade from auto upholstery to auto repairman because instead of going to Detroit, I had decided that I would return home upon completion of my training. I knew this guy back home who was about my age and was a master auto body repairman. He had a supped-up white Dodge Coronet that he had painted and modified (himself) in a manner that separated it from the rest of the hot rods in the area. I decided that I would not go to Detroit but instead, return home as an auto body repairman, make good money and building a mean street machine.

Training to be an auto body repairman proved to be much more difficult that I'd expected but I was determined not to give up. The center not only was obligated to teach corpsmen a trade but improve them academically as well. In high school, I was an attention-seeking jerk who was out to impress the girls but at the center there was no one to impress, except the teachers in the classroom. They were all male and my attempts to impress them were totally different than my motive for trying to impress the young ladies in high school. Having no distractions, I wanted to demonstrate my ability to learn in the classroom and I succeeded. The math teacher, Mr. James, was so impressed with me that whenever I was in his classroom, he never got up from his desk. Instead, he turned his classroom over to me and being only 19, this was a serious boost to my self-esteem. The math, for me, was not difficult but most of the students in the class had not graduated high school, nor did they have a GED. I looked forward to teaching the class each day, but I hated the auto body repair training.

At the end of the day, I would return to the dorm and (radio) listen to music or write letters (we had no TV). Every now and then, a problem would surface in the dorm between the corpsmen and I would have to step in and mediate a peaceful solution, which usually resulted well…

but this was not always easy. My first test of nerve as dorm leader came when I had to rescue a white guy living in my dorm room. Three black guys from other dorms were trying to take advantage him. They had sold him a watch for $10 (due on payday) that was not working. He was the only white guy in my dorm and the guys that were trying to take advantage of him were all black. In fact, most of the guys at the center were black and it was not uncommon to see a group black corpsmen beating up on one white guy. Even to this day, the image of this one poor white guy bleeding from being punched, slapped and kicked still bothers me. I never really knew the reason for the beating but I knew it was wrong for four or five guys to beat up on one helpless individual. I later heard that the victim had referred to some black person as "nigger," which was about as close as committing suicide as one could come in those days, under the circumstances. Blacks outnumbered whites by a ratio of approximately 10 to 1, or more. Mexicans were the second largest ethnic group at the center and seldom did I witness any of them being "jumped" by a group of blacks. The one incident that I did witness, it was not as lopsided as I'd witnessed whenever black guys attacked white corpsmen. This Mexican guy was out numbered three to one and although he was bloodied, he held his own and did never made any attempt to run.

It was payday and this night three black guys came into the dorm demanding money from A guy for the broken watch they'd sold him. When he tried to explain to them that it was did not work they threatened to beat him up. At that point, I came out of my room and demanded they leave him alone and get out. To my amazement, they left him alone and for the remainder of his stay at the center, never bothered him again. Needless to say, I became his closest ally and no one bothered or took advantage of him again... except me. A guy had this habit of borrowing money from me with the promise of paying it back with 50% interest. For every $5 he borrowed, he would give me a return of $7.50, which was not bad (for me), since my bi-weekly pay had been increased to $22.50. At first I felt guilty for taking the extra $2.50 but then I thought about the fact that not only was he begging me to make the deal, I was also protecting him from the wolves on base that would take his money and give him nothing in return, except a beating if he failed to comply.

It wasn't long before word started to circulate throughout Blue Block that I would loan money at an interest rate of 50 percent, payment due bi-weekly, on payday. Some guys were paying me 100 percent interest and never complained. Although JC was paying me only $22.50 every two weeks, it was not uncommon for me to make $50 or $60 in interest alone, which afforded me many of the luxuries that most other corpsmen did not have. With these luxuries, came an unprecedented degree of respect. Of course, the center's staff was not aware of my money-making scheme.

I'll never forget the weekend I went to San Antonio and purchased this small portable record player I'd put on lay-a-way weeks earlier. I think I paid $22 dollars for it at the time but anyway, on the way back to the center one could hear a pin drop...as everyone was listening to the tunes of Marvin Gaye. Not only could I afford to buy music but my own personal clothes as well. The Job Corps was the best thing that had ever happened to me because I was young and fancy-free. I had no love or emotional attachments to anyone and I was free to roam the streets of the big cities on weekends with money to spend. All this was during a time when, "Does Anybody Know What Time It Is" was blaring on the radio and I loved to sing along with the lyrics, "Does Anyone Really Care?" I can remember feeling so free at the time that while strolling down the streets of San Antonio, couldn't help but sing, "Oh No. I Don't Care What Time It Is." It was the best time of my life but it would be short-lived, although I would spend many years trying to recapture the evasive Cloud 9 experience.

I served as dorm leader for approximately five months, of which four of those months were named "Dorm of the Month." This meant that everyone in the dorm was treated to a steak dinner and given a certificate signed by the center's director. My dorm manager would always tell me how proud of me he was for our achievements. It was during this time that I first began to believe that I was born to lead. I didn't have enough sense or enough knowledge of God at the time to give Him the credit. Instead, I gave the credit to my mother. There were several years when I was without a father or male figure in the home and mother had to work to support the family. She would often have to walk approximately two miles (round trip) to iron clothes and clean house for $2 or $3 a day. Many of those trips were during the summer months when it was 90 degrees or higher. I don't recall her ever having an umbrella to protect her from the sun but I do remember her having to make the journey on foot while pregnant.

While she was away during the day, I was in charge of the house. If anything went wrong while she was away, I was the one that had to answer. She left my six or seven siblings and the house to my charge. I had to always be on the alert because if anything got out of order, then it was up to me to put things back in order before she returned home from work. This was during the early 60's and we had no telephone, therefore, we could not afford to have emergencies that could not wait until she returned home. If I could have prevented the emergency, then I had to answer for it. If a problem was due to one of my siblings being disobedient, then he or she had to answer. The government did not interfere with the training of children as they do today. Back then we were whipped with switches, branches, belts and pretty much whatever else was within reach. We bore welts and bruises but they always healed and 90% of the time...were well deserved. The 10% we received that was undeserved (at the time), we counted as deserved during the times we should have been whipped... but escaped punishment.

Being a dorm leader, I was stern but flexible. I knew when a fellow corpsman was giving his best efforts to follow the dorm rules and I knew when someone was testing my authority. I never backed down from anyone and I never got into a physical altercation while at the center. I treated everyone the same, having no respect of person. After my friend left for the Air Force, I felt alone at times. I didn't even a girlfriend but all that was about to change. We were allowed to take a one or two-week leave after being enlisted in the Job Corps for six months and most guys went back home to visit as soon as they became eligible...

but not me. When I became eligible for leave, I remained at the center because I had called my mother every two weeks since arriving at the center and I had no love interest back home. However, I was corresponding with a few friends, both male and female every week. Approximately, seven months after being in the Job Corps, I received a letter from a female friend, telling me that a friend of hers wanted to meet me. Her friend's name was the same as my best friend's (the one in the Air Force) sister, so I thought that's whom my female friend was referring to.

I had no romantic interest in my friend's sister but I did like her and besides, she was the best friend of the girl that had broken my heart and caused me to leave home in the first place. So, I decided to write her a letter and when she responded indicating that she might be interest in more than a friendship, I wrote back indicating the same. A week or so after we started exchanging letters, I dreamed that we were married. After corresponding for a month or so every week, I decided to take my leave and return home for two weeks. The corps purchased the round-trip ticket and may have even given me extra traveling money (can't recall) but I always kept money for loan sharking so I had more than enough to pay my own traveling expenses. When I left the center on leave that day, I had every intention of returning to complete my training as an auto repairman. I can't recall what I was thinking during the two-day journey back home but somewhere between the first letter from my friend's sister and the last, I develop an emotional attachment to her. I was gradually falling in love and based on some of the letters I'd received from her, she was feeling the same for me.

I only had the one-night stand with the mad man's daughter since arriving at the center and that proved to be too risky to try again. Besides, the guys in the surrounding cities despised corpsmen and the young women did not take us serious because they knew we would be around (on average) no longer than six months to a year. When I arrived home, I met with my family and engaged in the usual small talk but my mind was on getting to Pearson (Ga.) where my girlfriend was. Her father was a single parent and worked at night. Needless to say, I waited until night to visit her. That same night, I decided that I would be returning to Texas earlier than I had planned...but not to stay. I was returning to get my belongings so I come back home to be with my girlfriend. As for the auto body repairman training, I would either receive a certificate of completion, or I would leave without it. I certainly knew that I had not earned it but it didn't matter. I just wanted out of Job Corps...as soon as possible.

When I returned to the center, I told Lucas (the wake-up guy) that I was leaving. He looked at me with a smile and said, "Yeah, that girl done got to you." I didn't admit to it, nor did deny his claim. I just knew that I was leaving. Pops, the dorm manger, tried to talk me into staying but to no avail. My mind was made up and I was catching the earliest bus back to Willacoochee. My training instructor reluctantly issued me a signed Certificate of Completion, which meant that I would receive the $50 set aside for me each month I was at the center. I knew that I was not qualified to even train as an auto repairman but I wanted out. As promised, the center called and secured me a position at the Ford dealership in Douglas, Ga. I would be on-the-job training and that was fine with me. I really wanted to learn auto body repair but at the same time, I really wanted my freedom. While home on leave, I started to feel a freedom denied me by the Job Corps. Suddenly, the rules I had obeyed and enforced were now burdensome to me and I wanted to be free to do what I wanted to. Approximately, nine months after arriving at the Job Corps Center, I was on my way back to Willacoochee…with no viable plan for the future.

4

ON MY OWN

In less in a year, I had graduated high school, enlisted in the U. S. Army, gotten honorably discharged, joined the Job Corps and now was on my way back home...to live with my parents. I had no education and had refused to learn a trade that would have enable me to have a decent livelihood by having a decent job. I was in love and nothing else mattered. I simply decided to cross life bridges as I got to them, which didn't take long. Passing through Tifton, Ga., I looked out the (bus) window and saw a red 1966 Chevrolet Super Sport Impala 327, with a black vinyl top. I told the young lady sitting next to me that I was going to buy that car. She was also from Willacoochee and was returning home (I think) from Albany, Ga. She was a few years older than I and had flirted with and teased me during my senior year of high school. Now, I was all grown up and wanted to impress her...even though I had left the Job Corps because I'd fallen in love with someone else. The flirtation and my reaction was a sign of things to come.

Once back at my parent's home, it was made clear by my mother that I had to go to work and support myself. My step-father was stern but he never said too much to the kids but Mom was his spokesperson. The free ride for me was over and I was back on my own again. The Job Corps Placement Counselor had gotten me an on-the-job-training position at the Ford dealership in Douglas, Ga., in the auto body repair department. JC had agreed to pay my employer a certain percentage of my weekly salary. I had no transportation of my own but my uncle would drop me off at work in the morning (on his way to the same trailer plant that I'd walked away from a year earlier) but after work, I had to get back home the best way I could. It was not uncommon for me to walk several miles after work before being picked up by someone who lived in Willacoochee.

I knew next to nothing about auto body repair and this soon became obvious to the men assigned to train me. I had a "Auto Body Repair Certificate of Completion" but had not earned it...the same as I had not earned my high school diploma. I knew how to mix Bondo (putty/filler) and spread it on a dented panel but would often spent the entire day trying to sand it smooth. I couldn't mix paint and the ingredients were too expensive to train or experiment with. While training in Job Corps, it was okay to make mistakes because the government was paying for the supplies but in the real world, this employer did not tolerate mistakes, especially, when it came to losing money. I was the only black person in the shop but I never detected any signs of prejudice, although I was just not qualified to train for the job I'd been hired to do.

Unlike the Job Corps, there was no full-time trainer to teach me what I should have learned while at the center. The guys working in the shop had to make a living for themselves and therefore, started spending less time trying to train me. I started running more and more store errands for the shop supervisor, which had nothing to do with auto body repair. He would often send me to the store to purchase lemons (he loved to suck on lemons) and other food products for himself and the crew. When I wasn't running errands, I was sweeping the floor and cleaning the shop. I think they had given up on me and that was fine at first, so long as I was getting paid. But as the weeks went by, I noticed a change in the way the supervisor and the others would ask me to do things.

The gentle requests to bring something to a worker in the shop, or to make my daily "lemon run" changed to yelling and demands. Whenever asked to bring a certain tool and I brought the wrong tool, the guys would just shake their head and laughed...as if I was the dumbest thing this side of the Mississippi. Being the only black person in the shop, I convinced myself that I was being made fun of because of my race. I started to feel as if I was their "boy" and that they expected me to bow down before them because they were white. I ignored the fact that I had been given an opportunity to learn the same trade they were employed to perform...but had refused to do so. I clocked out one evening and never went back, except to get my paycheck. Now I was right back where I was a year prior, staying with my parents and out of work...only now I was more frightened than ever because I had gotten a taste of what being on my own was really like. I wanted to return to JC but I was in love and feared that if I left, someone would take my girl; therefore, going back was not an option. I decided to return (part-time) at the local sawmill so I could earn enough money to pay for my stay at my parent's home.

I worked at the sawmill for two or three week before being hired at the textile mill in Nashville, Ga. Several people from Willacoochee were employed there so getting to and from work was not a problem. My biggest problem was staying awake on the job. I had been hired to work the 12-hour graveyard shift and I was not getting my proper rest during the day. On one occasion, a friend and I did not have a ride home after working all night so we left walking and hitchhiking, trying to get home. After we had walked three or four miles we decided to lie down and take a nap beside the road. It was a crazy ideal but we were both tired and sleepy. As I started to doze off, someone kicked my foot. I looked up and it was a state trooper. He said someone had reported seeing us lying beside the road and thought we were dead. After explaining our ordeal, he stated that he understood but that we would have to move on. A few days later, the money set aside each month I was in JC arrived and I was about to purchase my first car.

My uncle, yes, the same one I disappointed at the trailer plant, took me to Nashville, Ga. to get a car. I wanted to go to Tifton and get the 1966 Super Sport I'd seen a few months earlier but he had established credit at dealership in Nashville therefore, that's where he took me because I had no credit. On the lot was a sleek red (maroon) 1966 Ford Galaxy 500 XL with leather bucket seats, air conditioning and a 390 engine. Man, this car was sharp! I fell in love with it the moment I saw it. My uncle drove it around the block and then assured me that it was a good car and that I should get it. I handed the salesman a down payment of $300 and my uncle signed the finance papers. I didn't know the total cost of the car, nor did I know what the monthly payments would be. I'm sure I was told but I didn't hear. I was just glad to have a ride...and a sharp ride at that! Now I could visit my girlfriend whenever I wanted; and I could also hang with the guys who had nice rides, and I would be able to and from work...in that order.

My duties at the textile mill were not strenuous but the 12-hour graveyard shift, I hated. I was tired of taking NoDoz pills, which kept me awake on the job but made me extremely nervous. I was finding it very difficult to sleep during the day time and besides, I could not visit my girlfriend like I wanted to. I was scheduled to work one night when my car got stuck in the woods (really should not have been there) and I had to walk back to town. I called my supervisor and told him I was having car problems and he informed me that if I could not be there at the start of the shift to not worry about coming in that night. I took this to mean that I was fired and therefore, did not go back to the mill except to get my paycheck. When he saw me, he asked why I had not returned to work and I explained to him that I thought he had fired me. He stated that he had not fired me. He had simply gotten someone else to work in my place that night. I did not ask to be rehired because I had already returned to the sawmill, working just enough to pay room and board (again) and buy gas so I could visit my girlfriend...and race my car. I was 19 years old at the time and had no sense of responsibility. I wanted to hang with the big dogs when it came to racing, although, I was a Chihuahua in the sport of racing. This was during the early 70's and drag racing was the main past time in Willacoochee. The guys would take their muscle cars (and trucks) down on Springhead Highway and race the quarter mile. Some would race on top end (one mile) but most ran the quarter. My car was not built for racing but I made it a racecar anyway.

I managed to buy two rear chrome wheels but could not afford the air shocks needed to heist the rear end of the car. So, I took several 2x4 wooden blocks and placed them between the rear springs to lift the rear. This created a very bumpy ride but gave the appearance of a "souped-up" racecar...at least, in my mind. I wanted white lettered tires but could not afford them, so I took white paint and attempted to write "Good Year" on the tires. I soon realized just how ridiculous that was and abandoned the idea but I still did something that was probably just as ridiculous. After installing an 8-Track player in the car, I connected two rear trailer (mobile home) lights to its wires so that they blinked to the beat of the music. Man, that was cool! It was country...but it was cool.

A classmate and I went job hunting one day and got a job working for a construction company. Just so happened they were doing work in the parking lot of a poultry plant in Douglas, Ga. We decided, after a few hours of sweating at the end of a shovel, to go inside and apply for employment. We were both hired on the spot and started work the next evening. Of course, I didn't like my job duties at the poultry plant, nor did I like working the 3 p.m. to 11:00 p.m. evening shift. My classmate depended on me to give him a ride to and from work but he soon discovered that I was not reliable. I would often call in and inform the supervisor that I would not be in (for one reason or another), thus leaving my classmate having to get to work the best way he could. I was young, wild and thought I was in love but by no means committed to work or girl. When I wasn't at work or with my girlfriend, I was often in "other" places. One of those "other" places resulted in me being chased through the streets of Willacoochee at midnight by an angry boyfriend who was accusing me of double-crossing him by sleeping with his girlfriend. I had a Saturday Night Special (.22 revolver) but no ammunition. I was finally able to stop running long enough to get out the car and knock on the door of a guy who gave me ammo. That ended the pursuit. A few days later, I confronted my pursuer, with gun visible in waistband, to resolve the matter. We both agreed to let it go.

Nighttime was the right time for me to party, or do whatever I wanted. I eventually just stopped calling in to work at the poultry plant and only returned to, you got it, get my paycheck. I had my priorities all in the wrong place and working was nowhere near the top of the list. The only time I could see my girlfriend was at night, while her father was at work out of town. I never asked his permission to date her, or to be in his house when he wasn't there. I just did it. I was arrogant, selfish and starting to get angry...at the world. Somehow, I had come to believe that life was one big party and that I could enjoy life without working. I did not like the idea of having to be at a certain place, at a certain time; nor did I like the type of work available to me and I definitely did not like anybody telling me what to do. The longest stint I had worked a full-time job since graduating high school was two months. I was on my own again and I hated it.

5

RUNNING AWAY

On Thanksgiving Day in 1971, I invited my girlfriend to come and have dinner with me and my family. I don't know if her father was aware that she was dating me or not but he allowed her to borrow his car. I'm not sure as to how it all happened but she and I end up racing around a corner in Willacoochee, with her being on the wrong side of the road. When I saw this, I felt something bad was about to happen…and it did. She met another car on the curve and was hit on the passenger's side, forcing her dad's car into the ditch. Thinking she had been seriously injured, I jumped out of my car and rushed over and yanked her door open. She was not injured but afraid of what her father would do to her for wrecking his car. She was crying and screaming, "He's going to kill me!" I didn't take her words literally but I thought he might whip her for sure. Besides, I' wasn't even sure he knew where she was going when he gave her permission to borrow the car. Nevertheless, being unable to think straight, I helped her into my car and we fled the scene of the accident.

I parked in the nearby woods and we remained there for several hours until it was dark. I then I walked back to town and found a friend who gave me $20 for food and gas.

After handing me two Black Beauty Pills (amphetamines), he informed me that a lady had been injured in the wreck but he didn't know how badly. He only knew she had been taken away by ambulance. I thought the worst because I knew we had caused the accident. In addition, I had fled the scene, so I knew I was facing serious jail time. To ease my fears, I took both of the pills my friend had given me. I'd take Black Beauty pills in the past and knew they not only gave you a feeling of well-being, but one pill would keep you awake and alert for at least 12 hours or longer…but I'd never before taken two at the same time.

It was cold and my girlfriend and I needed shelter, at least for the night. I went to a relative's house that lived in the country and asked if we could spend the night but she was afraid and said no. She instead, encouraged me to stop running before someone got hurt but when she realized I was not going to surrender to law enforcement, she gave me $20 and we left. Not really knowing where to go or what to do, I came back to Willacoochee under the cover of darkness and headed towards Coffee County. But while driving to Douglas, my girlfriend's aunt spotted us and started to follow. I tried to outrun her and when that failed, I made a quick U-turn and fled in the opposite direction. We ended up in Waycross, Ga., where we spent the next two days. Honeymooning was the last thing on my mind because I knew that I had to return, sooner or later, and face the music but I needed time to think. I thought about going to South Florida where my father was but then I thought about my girlfriend being underage, which would have only resulted in another serious charge. I was now twenty years old and she was only seventeen. I knew that crossing the state line with a minor could result in prison time, not to mention being charged and convicted of Statutory Rape. I explained this to my girlfriend but at the same time, assured her that we would not return if she didn't want to. She agreed that we should surrender to law enforcement, so we did.

We went to the authorities in Waycross but to my amazement, they wanted nothing to do with us. I think they checked to see if we were wanted by the police but I'm not sure. However, I *am* sure that they suggested we turn ourselves in at State Patrol office in Douglas. During the ride to Coffee County, my girlfriend and I barely said a word to each other. I don't know what she was thinking but I was wondering how much jail time I would receive. But feeling macho and defiant, I had no regrets about anything that had happened over the past three days because life had been so unfair to me. To survive, I had been forced to work jobs that I hated, even working during hours when I should have been sleeping. If that's what life was all about then I didn't see how I was going to make it anyhow, so my attitude towards being punished was, "Bring it on." After about 45 minutes of driving, we arrived in Douglas.

As soon as we stepped into the Georgia State Patrol office, I told them who we were and why we were there. An officer immediately yelled, "Take that hat off inside this building, Boy!" He then got in my face so close that his nose almost touched mine. Looking me in the eye, he said the woman involved in the accident had broken her foot and that I was lucky that no one had gotten seriously injured or killed. He then stated, "You'd better be glad that accident was the other people's fault" and I thought to myself,

"What?" The other people had actually been charged with causing the accident. They were totally innocent! At least, now I didn't have that to worry about being charged with "Hit and Run." Instead, we were charged with "Leaving the Scene of an Accident," which meant my license would be suspended for at least one year and I would have to pay a fine. A real slap on the wrist.

The Douglas authorities called for the Atkinson County Sheriff Department to come pick me up and to notify my girlfriend's father that we had been found. When the Atkinson County deputy arrived, my girlfriend's father was with him. The patrolman that had gotten in my face said to the father, "Wait til you hear where they been the last two days." He then looked at me and demanded, "Tell him!" Without hesitation, I said, "A hotel." Her father then said he would drive my car to the courthouse and added, "Where he's going to need it." I was put in handcuffs and placed in the back of the sheriff's cruiser and my girlfriend rode back to Pearson with her father. I was sure the father was going to file charges of Statutory Rape against me but to my surprise...he didn't.

After arriving at the Pearson courthouse, I watched as my girlfriend's father gently closed my door after making sure that the windows were rolled up. I wondered why he did not slam the door in anger, and why it mattered to him whether or not the windows were up. He obviously was not the monster I'd made him out to be. Nevertheless, I was taken to a cell and locked up for five or six hours, until a friend came and paid the $50 fine. It was my first time being in jail and I hoped it would be the last but I was not afraid to go back to jail. Upon my release, I was warned by the local authorities not to return to my girlfriend's house, or else I would go to jail for a very long time.

Things were relatively calm when I arrived at my mother's house that evening but early the next morning, she started to scold me for what I'd done and for not having a job. I didn't want to hear what she was saying and I didn't want to talk to anyone about anything. I left the house walking, not knowing or caring where I was going. I started walking south on the railroad tracks and the next thing I remembered was awakening in the Douglas hospital. I was mentally and physically exhausted. I had taken those two Black Beauty pills the day of the accident to stay awake and alert. To sleep, I had taken two sleeping pills when I returned home the day before. When I awaken in the hospital, I saw people reading a letter (I had on me) that I'd written to my girlfriend's brother, who was in the Air Force, stationed in California. I was really embarrassed to know people were actually reading my thoughts. The sheriff took the letter and kept it as evidence. After that incident, realizing I could not explain being found passed out on the side of the highway due to the mixture of drugs (uppers & downers), I realized that I had to leave Willacoocheee...forever!

6

LIVING ON THE EDGE

Humiliated and embarrassed by leaving the scene of the accident, as if I was rescuing my girl from the rails of an oncoming train and later ending up passed out on the side of the road due to drugs and exhaustion, I felt like a sore, swollen thumb. I knew everywhere I went, people would be thinking about what happened; therefore, I felt a need to erase the incident from their mind all that had happened on Thanksgiving Day and the days that followed. Not only had the letter I wrote to my girlfriend been read by law enforcement, but several other town folks as well. Now, my thought would be exposed to the public and I had to find some way to re-establish myself as a tough guy. The letter had revealed the tender side of me. I went back to work at the local sawmill, but still only working part-time. My mother made it clear that I had to pay to stay in their home or else I would have to move out. I still had not accepted the fact that I was an adult and nobody was going to give me anything. I had no other choice but to pay for a place to stay but I still felt that my parents were somewhat responsible for taking care of me.

I tried to fit in with the local people by racing the guys who had purchased vehicles for the sole purpose of racing.

I was not making payments on my car, nor was I keeping up the maintenance on it. It wasn't long after I started racing that the radiator started to leak but having no money to replace it, I continue to drive and race. A week or so later, the transmission started to go bad. Occasionally, the car would jump into reverse when I started it. This was the beginning of the end of what was once a very nice automobile. I didn't realize how nice it was, until it started to go bad. It was my first car and I didn't know how to appreciate it. Like everything else, I took it for granted.

Both law enforcement and my girlfriend's father had forbidden me to see her but as usual, I was defiant. I continued to see her but was no longer parking my car at the apartment. Instead, I parked in what I thought was an abandoned road and would walk he short distant to the apartment. One night while visiting her, there was a knock on the door. I was not afraid because I knew if it was her father, he would not be knocking and I knew it was not law enforcement because they didn't know I was there. When my girlfriend opened the door, I was surprised to see that it was ex-girlfriend. She was there not to start trouble, but rather to inform me that my car was being towed by the police.

I rushed down to where I had parked and was met by law enforcement. After asking if it was my car and me confirming that it was, they asked to see my license, which I didn't have because they had been suspended because of the of the accident. The police informed me that I was illegally blocking a road and because my license was suspended they would have to tow the car. An officer asked if the car would start and I said yes. I watched as he got inside and started it up, while another officer stood between the rear of my car and the front of a cruiser. I remember hoping the car would jump into reverse, as it occasionally did, and crush the officer's legs. But by the Grace of God, it did not. I'm not sure I was so angry with law enforcement. They had done nothing but show me kindness when they could have taken me to jail...on more than one occasion.

Although I was working at the sawmill and could have paid the $44 towing and compound charges, I refused to do so. Not only was it in serious need of repair, it was also now well known by law enforcement; therefore, I decided to just abandon it. I never took into consideration that my uncle had co-signed for me to get the car; nor did I care about his credit being ruined. I was only concerned about me. A few weeks after the car was towed, two men approached me while I was fishing at a local creek with a guy whose kindness I would later take advantage of. These men had come to repossess the car. I told them where it was and they asked me to accompany them to the sheriff department, which I did...but not before borrowing the $44 from my fishing partner to have the car released from compound. After paying the fee to have the car released, I was told by a deputy sheriff that I did not have to pay to have the car released because the dealership would've paid. There's no way I would have paid the charges had I had known that beforehand. Nevertheless, I wouldn't be without a car for long.

That 1966 Chevrolet Super Sport Impala with the black vinyl top and chrome rims that I'd saw in Tifton (on my way home from the Job Corps) appeared before me like a bright light and I wondered if it was still there. Within two months, I had managed to save $300 and was now ready to purchase another car. The first place I checked was the lot where I had seen the 66 Impala and to my amazement, it was still there. I took that as a sign meaning it had remained unsold all those months because it was meant for me. It never crossed my mind that it might still be on the lot because it had seen its best days and therefore, not worth the asking price. I'm not sure it would have made a difference either way because I just wanted to fit in with the racing crowd. The car was sharp and that's all that really mattered to me. I just wanted to get it home, clean it up and show it off but there was just one problem. I needed a co-signer. I had burned the bridge that once linked my uncle and I, so I knew he would not co-sign on a loan with me again.

I asked the kind guy whom I had been fishing with when my car was repossessed if he would co-sign with me to get the 66 Impala and he without hesitation, agreed to do so. It was late in the evening when he and I returned to the dealership to purchase the car. After the salesman jump started it (I had never so much as listen to the sound of the engine or test driven the car), I eager to get behind the wheel and wrestle with the 4-speed manual transmission. I was not very familiar with shifting gears but it didn't matter. I had to have this car because it would make me somebody of the hometown people. I needed it to help erase the events surrounding the accident from their mind.

As I was driving back home, I imagined racing across the quarter mile bridge just outside the Willacoochee city limits. To get a feel of what it would be like, I decided to take a different route. From Tifton, I drove to Nashville and from there to Willacoochee. A few miles before I reached the quarter mile bridge, I was running 90 miles per hour. But a mile or so before I got there, an inaudible voice said, "Slow Down." Just before I reached the bridge, I slowed down to approx. 60 miles per hour and as soon as I got onto the bridge, the front right tire came off, causing the car to swerve violently from one side of the bridge to the other...but it never touched its sides. Once the car was off the bridge, I steered it to the side of the road and come to a complete stop...avoiding the steep embankment below.

When I got out and looked at the car I could see that the front right fender was heavily damage and the tire was nowhere to be found. I left the car and walked the approximately 1 ½ mile home. Early the next morning, I was able to locate and remount the lost tire. I checked and discovered the lug nuts on the other three tires were loose and the tires about to come off as well. I was able to turn most of the lug nuts on the wheels with my hand. The tires had been mounted on the car with regular lug nuts, although the wheels (rims) were chrome mags and required special lug nuts. I drove the car home and had every intention of having it repaired...but after getting fired from the sawmill, I unable to do so. Needless to say, this car too was repossessed but not without an attempt by the dealership to collect payment.

While sitting outside listening to music, a man identifying himself as the sheriff of Tift County paid me a visit and demanded I pay for the car. I informed him that I was not paying for a car that was wrecked because they [dealership] didn't used the proper lug nuts bolts on the tires. He just said, "Well, you need to pay for that car."

And he turned and walked away. I never heard anything else from the dealership or anyone else about the car. Not even the guy who had co-signed for the loan bothered to mention it. Of course, it would have made no difference if he had; although, I'm sure the repossession had a negative impact on his credit. Now I was without a job and a car and no way to visit my girlfriend where there's a will... there's a way.

7

30-DAY NOTICE

I did not the like the idea of working so, I never kept a steady job for more than a few days, a few weeks, or a few months. After being fired at the sawmill, I was hired at another trailer plant in Douglas. I had no transportation of my own so I had to catch a ride with three other guys from Willacoochee that worked at the same place. I was hired as a "finisher" because I told the employer that I had experience in building trailers. Since I had previously been hired and worked one day at the first trailer plant (the day after graduation), I thought that alone would qualify me as being experienced. Unlike my first experience at the trailer plant, the work was not nearly as burdensome but I was at a total lost as to what to do…and there was no one there to train me. Nevertheless, I was expected to do the job. I knew nothing about how to read a tape measurer, use a skilled saw, or even a properly use a hammer to drive a nail. I was just there but I was trying.

A few minutes before the shift ended one day, I was in the bathroom trying to get debris out my eye when the supervisor walked in. He didn't say anything but immediately turned and walked back out. When I clocked out at the end of the shift, he told me I was wanted in the office. I didn't really know what it was about but thought I was about to be reassigned a new position but I was wrong. After being informed that I had been on the job for two weeks and had not met the company's expectation, I was being "let go." I literally pleaded with the men in the office to give me more time...but to no avail. The fact that I was wearing a cap every day, bearing a hand-drawn "Black Panther Party" symbol probably didn't help my case any. It was 1972 in South Georgia and the idea of anyone, especially a young black man, showing support for black militant organization such as the Black Panther Party was not received well. I'd always been somewhat radical when it came to race issues but never entertained the thought of becoming militant.

The thing I admired most about the Black Panthers was the black berets they wore. I was never impressed by their guns and purpose because I knew they were no match for white America. They had assault rifles and pistols but the government had tanks and bazookas, and wiretaps, and black informants, and the right to use these weapons. Oh yeah, I also admired Angela Davis, a black female who had close relations with Black Panther Party. My admiration for Ms. Davis had nothing to do with her affiliation with the Civil Rights Movement. It was because I thought she was pretty.

The guys were waiting for me in the car and I could tell by the look on their faces that they knew I had been fired; nevertheless, I told them I had been laid off. During the 20-mile trip home, everyone was silent, as if they could feel my pain. I tried hard not to cry but couldn't keep the tears from streaming down my face. I just let them flow, making no attempt to wipe them away because I didn't want the guys to notice me crying. When I got home, I told my mother what happened and she was very understanding, realizing that some jobs were not for everybody...but I was still expected to get a job and I didn't have to look far. Two weeks after being fired from the trailer plant in Douglas, I was hired at a trailer plant in Pearson. I told the employer that I had experience as a "finisher," since that was my job title at the last plant I'd worked. He seemed excited to have me aboard and after explaining the benefits, he introduced me to the plant foreman who put me to work. At the end of the shift, I was escorted to the office and told by my employer that they had made a mistake in hiring me because they really did not need another Finisher. This time, I did not beg. I just said, "Thank you" and left.

My brother helped me get a job at the local Jon Boat company where he worked and believe it or not, I was hired as "finisher." Unlike the trailer plant, finishing boats easy. My duties involved using a roller to smooth fiberglass, a brush to paint, and adding metal molding along the edges of the boat with a rivet gun. Not only was this job within walking distance, it was actually fun because I could be creative. There were only four or five guys working there at any given time and two of those guys were sons of the company owner. The work environment was friendly, except on those occasions when the brothers would get into a small altercation (mostly shoving matches), and my brother and I would have to separate them. The job didn't pay very much but it kept Mom off my back. But I still needed a ride of my own so I could visit my girlfriend eleven miles away.

The eldest son of my employer was the supervisor but he was down to earth and friendly. He also had an interest in racing. He drove a nice 1970 Chevy El Camino but it was not considered a hot rod because it had air conditioning. So, he purchased a 1955 Chevrolet that had been modified for racing. This Mean Green Machine was cool...but cumbersome and not fit for every day transportation. It had a modified engine, 4-barrel carburetor, 4-speed transmission, chrome rims, and it was high off the ground. I liken it to a hayride on a wagon in a bumpy field. Since having my first car repossessed, I'd relied on others for a ride to go see my girlfriend. My brother's girlfriend lived in town, so he would sometimes let me borrow his car; although, I had no valid driver's license. At other times, I would catch a ride with someone going to Pearson and get back the best way I could.

On more than one occasion, I actually walked the eleven miles back home after midnight. It usually took 2 ½ hours of walking at a non-stop fast past get back home. But sometimes, rather than walk back home I would spend the night with my girlfriend and then slip out the next morning...with her father in the house. I would then hitchhike back to Willacoochee, sometimes walking several miles before getting a ride. One morning, I was picked up and given a ride by a deputy sheriff that knew I had been visiting my girlfriend. Although he knew I had been forbidden to see her, he was very kind (as usual) and we just talked about things in general.

During the ride, I asked him if it was illegal to carry a handgun and he told me that it was. I wanted to tell him about the loaded .22 caliber revolver in my right front pocket but decided not to. I had the gun with me in case my girlfriend's father caught me in his house. The plan was to kill him, my girlfriend, and myself. I knew he had a gun and would probably use it and I had no intention of going to prison. As for my girlfriend, if I couldn't have her, then nobody would. Of course, she knew nothing of my plan.

My boss's son decided that he no longer wanted to invest time or money in the 55' Chevy, so I persuaded him to sell it to me. I couldn't afford it but I really wanted it. I was more concerned with racing than I was with having adequate transportation because the car had no (working) lights at the time and the gears were very difficult to shift due to a bad clutch, or a bad transmission...I was told. But even if the gears had been in perfect working order, it would have made very little difference because I barely knew how to drive a "standard shift" vehicle. Nevertheless, I decided that I would deal with all those problems once I got the car. The son agreed to sell me the car for $500 and I thought that was a real bargain. I looked beyond everything that was wrong with it and visualized racing the quarter mile with the guys who had racecars they could afford (payments and maintenance). I could not so much as afford a down payment on the asking price. The owner of the boat plant agreed to co-sign the $500 loan with me at the bank and it was a done deal. A local "shade tree" mechanic agreed to repair the lights in exchange for the two rear chrome rims and within 30 minutes, he had the lights functioning (by replacing a fuse) and I was out of two chrome rims. The next task was getting the gears shifting smoothly, which proved impossible. Within two weeks, I had lost all interest in the car and therefore, decided I was not going to pay for it.

It was now the fall of 1972 and the demand for Jon Boats was on the declined. I was eventually laid off and I had no means of seeking employment. I had burned the bridge at the local sawmill and there were no other local employers hiring at the time; therefore, I hung around the house all day while my parents worked. After two or three weeks of doing nothing but eating and sleeping, my mother gave me an ultimatum. I had to have a job within 30 days, or else I would have to move out.

8

HOMELESS

For the first time in my adult life, I was serious about finding and keeping a job but I had burned too many bridges. No place I applied for employment would hire me. I even tried to get rehired at the textile mill after catching a ride to Nashville without having a way to get back. I ended up walking at least 9 of the 18 miles back home. Now, after being given the ultimatum, I was willing to accept any type of employment available. I just needed to go to work because I did not want to be without a place to lay my head. Unfortunately, when the 30 days were up, I could no longer spend the night in my parent's house. When I wasn't spending the night with my girlfriend, I slept in my brother's abandoned car in the front yard but this would not last. After a week or so, the car was removed and the only place I had to stay at night…was with my girlfriend.

For three week, I hung around my parent's house in Willacoochee during the day and stayed with my girlfriend in Pearson at night. I think her father became suspicious because when I walked pass his room the next morning, his door would be open. Sometimes he would be up and in the bathroom when I slipped out, and sometimes he would be in the back yard, when I walked out the front door. Each morning, I would brace for whatever might happen. I kept the revolver with me, ready to carry out my plan if and when necessary. On those occasions when I walked out the front door, and he was in the back yard, I expected to hear him shout out to me or just put a bullet in my back… but not once was I ever afraid. One weekend night, after my girlfriend had gone out to a local club and returned to her room, he knocked on the door. I had entered through the window (the only time I had done so) because he was home. I thought he had heard me sneaking in.

When he knocked on the door, I slipped down between the bed and the wall with gun in hand. I just knew he was there to confront me but was not. He only scolded her for going to the club. When he was done talking and the door was closed, my girlfriend and I resumed doing what we were doing before he knocked on the door. The next morning, I got up and walked out. He was in bed, facing the hallway with his room door open, which was unusual. After three weeks of risking my life and my freedom, I finally caught a break.

It was Election Day in Atkinson County and the local sheriff was seeking reelection. It's no secret that votes were bought and paid for during that time but one had to be a registered voter to reap the benefits. I was not registered to vote but the "good ol' boy" system of the day did not require proof of registration. I lied about being a registered voter and was given $3 for my promise to vote for the man funding the campaign. After receiving the illicit funds, I went to one of the local juke joints and with the $3, gambled in a card game. When I tripled my money, I abruptly quit the game and walked out with $10 and some change. I decided that I would use a portion of my winnings to purchase a one-way bus ticket to Brunswick, Ga. I had spoken weeks earlier with a childhood neighbor who lived there and he had promised if I come, he would help me find employment. Win, Lose or draw...I had no other choice but to go.

After catching a ride to Pearson and spending the night with my girlfriend, I got up early and headed for the Trailways Bus Depot, carrying one piece of luggage. After purchasing the ticket, which cost $3 (I think) and armed with a physical address, I boarded the bus and was on my way to Brunswick. During the 3-hour trip, I had lots of time to reflect on my life. It was scary when I thought about how lost I was, and how I had no plans for the future. I didn't know where I was going in life...I was just going. When I arrived in Brunswick, I stepped off the bus with no sense of direction, so I just started walking. I didn't have a clue as to what direction to walk and I (instinctively) knew not to ask strangers for direction. After walking for approximately 20-30 minutes, I saw this Cherry Red 1970 Mustang Mach 1 parked at a house and I knew I had found the place where I would be staying. I knocked on the door and an elderly gentleman answered. I told him who I was and that my friend had invited me to come live with him until I could find a job and get my own place. The elderly man had me wait at the door while he went to get my friend and when I saw his face, I was relieved. I was not aware that my friend was renting a room but it didn't matter, so long as I had someplace to lay my head at night.

My friend and I shared his room and I slept on the sofa. Whenever he had female company, I had to sit it out in the living room section of the house...even if the visit was casual. While he was trying to shield his lady friends from me, I was wondering what in the house I could steal and pawn. Other than treating me like a stepchild, when the ladies came around, my friend was really good to me. He paid for all my food, as well as a movie ticket to see, "A friend of mine's Big Score." The first Saturday in Brunswick, I spend helping a relative of his install carpet. After crawling around on my knees for eight hours, I was tired and the next day every muscle in my body ached. I fully expected to be paid for my labor but no mention of pay was made. One week later, my friend's sister helped me get a job a shrimp processing plant where she worked.

I was eager to go to work and I worked enthusiastically, trying my best to appreciate and enjoy my assigned duties. But at the end of the day, I was really tired (probably due to my eagerness to impress the supervisor) and decided that I was not going back, not even to collect my one day paycheck. When my friend awoken me the next morning, I told him the supervisor had instructed me to stay home until I was over my cold. He did not question me and I was left alone in the house during the day...looking for things to steal.

I stole a lady's watch from my friend and pawned it. When he discovered it gone, I told him that my social security card had been stolen, as well as a few other personal items, which I never had. A few days later, I received a letter from my girlfriend, informing me that a guy was interested in buying the 55 Chevy. I had not made one payment on the car since having it financed at the bank but it was still in my possession (at my parent's house). I decided that I was going to sell it but first, I needed money to get back home. I thought about the .32 caliber revolver I had discovered underneath the mattress of the elderly gentleman who owned the home. The day after receiving the letter from my girlfriend, I decided to leave Brunswick. I stole the pistol and took it to the pawnshop where I sold it for $25. I used a portion of the cash to purchase a one-way bus ticket back to Willacoochee.

I knew I could not move back in with my parents, so again, I had to spend the nights with my girlfriend. Two or three days after I returned home, the guy wanting to purchase the car asked how much I wanted for it. I agreed to sell it for $200 plus an additional $20 if he wanted the two remaining chrome rims. He agreed to the deal and one week later, I waited outside the bank while he went inside to get the $220 to purchase a car from me...that I did not own.

9

ATLANTA

I knew sooner or later, the gun I'd stolen and pawned would be missed and the theft traced back to me; therefore, I had to keep moving. Realizing I had burned all my bridges in Willacoochee, and now in Brunswick (where I'd stolen and pawned the gun), I allowed "A friend of mine," a hometown acquaintance to talk me into going to Atlanta, Ga. with him to work in construction. He assured me that I would have a job once I got there. I gave half the money from the sale of the car to my girlfriend to keep for me and the other half I took with me to Atlanta.

The Army and Job Corps had both provided me with food and shelter but since leaving the latter, I had been on my own. The reality of life had finally begun to sink in and I realized that I wasn't prepared to face the world. Life challenges were confronting me on a daily basis now and it was frightening. I wished many times I had taken school serious and sought higher learning, especially while spending those nights in the abandoned car. I also wish I had stayed in the Army, or at least stayed in the Jobs Corp and learned a trade but it was too late. Not only were those doors now shut, they were locked as well. My only option was to pick up the pieces and try to put together a life for myself but it would be much easier said than done.

I took a bus to Atlanta with just a little over $100 in my pocket and the promise of a construction job when I arrive. I had no experience doing construction work but I figured anyone could dig a hole and/or used a sledgehammer. Not only that but I'd heard the guys who worked construction in the city made big bucks. But I didn't know the price a (physical) weakling like me would pay...to earn the big bucks. It was at night when I arrived in Atlanta and I was lost, with no sense of direction. I locked my few belongings in a bus depot locker and set out to find a hotel to spend the night. After having roamed the streets of Austin and San Antonio at night while in the Job Corps, I wasn't afraid but I was very cautious; therefore, I quickly checked into one of the nearby hotels for the night. I checked out around noon the next day and went straight to the bus depot to check on my things. Everything was just as I'd left it, so I left them there while I checked out the city. I wasn't about to walk around with luggage, which would have been the same as saying, "Hey, look at me. I'm new in the city." Although the buildings were tall, I knew better than to spend too much time staring up at them. I knew there were people on the street looking for people like me, who were new to city life and therefore, easy prey when it came to being victimized.

It was getting late in the evening and all I had was an address where my hometown buddy and another homeboy were staying. I had no clue as to how to catch a city bus to get to the address and I didn't want to pay for another night at the hotel, which would have left me with only a few dollars. Just I'm starting to get really concerned about where I would spend the night, a miracle happened. I looked across one of the busy city streets and standing on the other side, waiting for the pedestrian light to turn green, was a young man from Willacoochee. I think we saw each other about the same time and when we met, we greeted each with an embraced. He told me how glad he was to see me but I was thinking, "Man, you don't know what glad is." I told him where I needed to go and we both boarded a city bus and rode to College Parks, Ga. After riding 30 or so minutes, and then walking a few blocks, we finally arrived at the place I would call home for the next few weeks. The young man gave me a phone number where he could be reached and then he left.

After spending the night on a sofa, which would be my bed for the remainder of my stay at that resident, I was summoned early the next morning and informed that I had a job. As promised, my buddy had secured a construction job for me. It was Friday and I still had a chance to make a few bucks for the weekend. So off to work in the big city I went. The plan was that after work I would take a city bus to the depot and get my belongings. I would then take another bus to the home of my former elementary school principal (residing in Atlanta) and someone there would bring me back to College Park. The plan seemed perfect, except I had underestimated the strenuous labor required to do my job. After slinging a sledgehammer for two hours, I started to get a real taste of reality, as the few muscles I had started to ache and burn. This labor was much harder than what I'd experienced at the trailer plants back home… but I knew that if I didn't work, I didn't eat. Although I had to get out of my parent's house because I couldn't keep a job, I was never refused a meal. But now I was in the city and I was determined not to become one of the several homeless people I'd seen searching for food in trashcans, dumpsters or begging for change on the street corner.

After swinging 9 pounds of steel attached to the end of a 33-inch wooden handle (sledge hammer) for 2 hours, I was tired and experiencing aches and pains like never before. I didn't weigh a pound over 140 at the time. I remember thinking maybe the foreman would have mercy on me and give me something lighter to do. But I soon realized that every man had been assigned a specific task to at the job site to perform and was expected to carry his own load. My assigned duty was to drive wooden stakes into the (sometimes) unyielding soil. In the past, if I didn't like a job I simply walked away but now I was in the real world and walking away be the same as walking away from food and shelter. It was mid-September but the hot blistering Atlanta sun was not yet ready to yield to the cool days of autumn and as a result, I sweated profusely. For the first time in my life, I was beginning to really appreciate a 15-minute break, which took forever and a day to come. I had only been on the job for two hours and already I was as tired as if I'd been working eight. During the break, I sat on the ground with my back against a steel beam and was thinking, "Man, there has to be a better way [to make a living] than this." I knew I would have to work a 9 to 5 to survive but I was not physically (or mentally) fit to do this type of manual labor. It seemed like only 5 minutes into the 15-minute break, and again it was time to sling that 9-pound piece of steel.

During the 30-minute lunch break, I was much more interested in resting than eating. I was too tired to eat, which means I didn't feel like feeding myself because to do so I would have to lift my tired, aching, burning arm. Nevertheless, I knew I had to eat if I was to survive the day. I drank plenty water throughout the day because the more I lifted a cup of water, the less I had to lift the sledge hammer. Immediately after lunch, I broke the handle of the sledgehammer, and then another, and another, and then another. During the next four hours, I would take out four handles...but I wasn't mad about it. Although this short delay was unintentional, with each handle replacement came at least 10 minutes of rest. Also with each broken handle came a roar of laughter from the guys, including the foreman but I wasn't laughing. I wasn't even smiling. I was just hoping we would run out of handles but there were plenty on hand. At last, the eight hours of torment was finally over and I was free to go downtown Atlanta to get my clothes from the bus depot. I was dirty and I'm sure I didn't smell very well after sweating all day but it was useless to take a bath before going downtown because I didn't have a change of clothes at the house I was staying. My plans were to get my clothes from downtown, come back get ready to hit the streets with the other guys but my body had other plans.

I do not recall the bus ride to the depot, nor do I recall arriving at my former principal's home but I do remember sitting on the floor in her home. It was early in the evening and already I was dozing off. I remember the principal asking if I wanted to take a bath and I said no. I was too tired to realize that she was probably giving me a hint. While waiting for someone to come and take me back to College Park, I decided to lay on the floor and take a nap.

I remember the principal, in a very kind and gentle voice, trying to persuade me to get off the floor and get on the sofa but again I declined. The next thing I remembered was waking up the next morning and seeing the dirty spot on the carpet where I had slept through the night. I was really embarrassed but what could I say? I took a shower, changed clothes, ate a hearty breakfast and then I was on my way. But not everyone would be so generous during my brief stay in the big city. In fact, I was to about to understand how a person could actually stand on a street corner holding a, "Will Work for Food" sign and not be ashamed to do so.

I arrived back in College Park resident around 11:00 a.m. on Saturday to find the guys hung over from the night before. There was beer cans and trash strewn throughout the house, even in the bathroom. I was still tired and aching all over from slinging that sledge hammer and I really wanted to rest but I could not. The house had only three bedrooms and I was the (non-rent paying) fourth guy, which meant I had to sleep on a sofa in the living room. That first weekend was a nightmare but I couldn't complain because I wasn't paying rent. The guys paraded in and out the house, making noise as if I wasn't there on the sofa trying to sleep. I finally gave up on sleeping when a fight broke out in the house over something really trivia (A friend of mine didn't mind fighting. In fact, I think he enjoyed fighting). When it was evening, the guys all got dressed and left the house but partying was the last thing on my mind. All I wanted was a few hours of rest and sleep. Approximately, four hours into a deep sleep, I was awoken by one of the guys and a woman he'd brought to the house. I tried to go back to sleep but got up when the couple started to argue about something that was definitely not worthwhile.

Somehow the woman managed to pull me into their argument by asking me a question. I was tired and half asleep, otherwise, I would have just ignored her but I made the mistake of giving my opinion. The answer I gave was honest and unbiased but it just happened to be in her favor, which really angered the guy. I had known him since the day I came to Willacoochee, some 12 years earlier and it was a known fact that his Viet Nam experience had left him somewhat traumatized and somewhat mentally unstable. His instability became very obvious whenever he drank, which is exactly what he was doing that night. In addition to being unstable, he stood well over 6 feet and had approximately 225 lbs. of solid muscle clinging to his frame. Knowing I was no match for him, I grew very concerned when he diverted his attention from the woman and focused on me. Staring into my eyes he asked, "Why you turning against me and taking her side, when I took you in and gave you a place to stay?"

As I'm trying to explain to him that I was not taking sides but was only giving my opinion, I could see that he was not hearing me. I was only 5 feet, 10 ½ inches and at 140 pounds, just barely more than skin and bones at the time. I was concerned about the "one touch kill" technique he often boasted about learning in the Marine Corps. As he started to get louder, the woman made the mistake of (verbally) coming to my aid, which only fueled his anger. Now, in his mind, it was both she and I against him. Just as I'm starting to think things are going to end really bad for me, A friend of mine stepped through the door. No sooner than he realized what was happening he said to the big guy, "If you fight anybody, it's gonna to have to be me." That was the end of the whole matter. The lessoned learned that night was, if a man and his woman, wife or girlfriend is arguing, if at all possible...stay out of it by keeping your opinion to yourself.

The ex-Marine apologized to me, even offered his bed for me to lay on while he and his date continue to drink, smoke and talk. I promptly accepted the offer and must have fallen asleep immediately because the next thing I remembered was being awaken two hours later. The guy and his date were moving from the living room to the bedroom, which meant I had to move back to the living room. By now, there were more people in the house and some were sitting on my bed (sofa). I couldn't lie down until the party was over, which was around 4:30 a.m. I slept until 2:00 p.m. that Sunday evening. Sunday night was calm, as everyone rested up for Monday morning. I dreaded the thought of Monday morning because I knew that 9-pound steel was waiting for me. I didn't know it then but the day would come that I would wish for a sledgehammer to sling, just so I could get food to eat.

It seemed like no longer than I laid down that Sunday night and closed my eyes, Monday morning was knocking on the door. It was time to sling that sledgehammer again and I dreaded the thought. But to my surprise, when we arrived at the job site I was given a new assignment. It wasn't because the boss was having pity on me, it was because all the stakes had been driven on Friday. My new assignment was not nearly as demanding as was driving stakes into the ground but it was aggravating and sometimes downright demeaning. I was a "helper," which meant I did whatever was needed to help the more experience guys complete their assignment for the day. This was aggravating in the sense that I never knew what I would be doing until I was told by one of the guys to do something (everybody was my supervisor). Sometimes I would have to dig a hole, fill a hole, carry lumber, steel rods or help hold the lumber and steel in place to be nailed or welded. The job became demeaning when the guys, including the supervisor, would heat up one end of a steel rod (without my knowledge) and hand me the heated section to hold. Everybody would have a good laugh at my reaction and I would play it off as if it was no big deal...because fighting was not an option. Besides, I needed a place to stay after work. Nevertheless, I never stopped looking for ways to get revenge and I would eventually find it before I left the city.

At the end of the week, I received a check for $350.00, the most I'd ever receive for a week's work. This was 1972 and that kind of money could go a long way, even in the city, if handled properly. Needless to say, I didn't know how to manage money and therefore, barely had enough to get me through the following week. After receiving the huge paycheck, it was party time and party I did. I spent money that weekend like I had a machine to print more. I was partying Friday night, Saturday night and late into Sunday evening (actually, early Monday morning). Even after all the guys had laid their bodies down to rest for the next day, I was still partying. When the foreman came to pick us up for work on Monday, I informed him that I would not be going that day. He said, "Okay" and then drove off with the other guys. I laid around all day Monday trying to rest up for the next day's work but to my amazement, there would be no work for me the next day. I got up early Tuesday morning, mentally and physically prepared to go to work but when the foreman arrived to pick up the other guys he said to me, "I don't have anything for you to do today." I didn't think too much about it and said, "Okay." I was actually glad because I wanted another day of doing nothing. However, when he gave me the same line the following day, and then the next, I realized that he had very politely fired me.

Realizing that I was going to be short of money, I called and had my girlfriend mail me the remainder of the money from the sale of the car. The money arrived on Saturday and when the guy pushed the envelope thru the top of the bathroom door, it landed on top of the open toilet seat. It was a sign of things to come, only my luck would not be quite as good. A friend of mine had always looked out for me and I wasn't surprised that he was asking the foreman (daily) why I wasn't working. The foreman continued to feed him the same line about me not being needed. This game went on for the entire week but that weekend, A friend of mine assured me that if I didn't go back to work on Monday, then neither would he. Not only was he a skillful laborer, he was also much needed on the job.

When Monday morning came, the foreman came to pick up the guys and I was standing outside with them, dressed and ready to go to work. A friend of mine asked if he had any work for me and he said no. A friend of mine then stated, "Well, if he don't work, I don't work. If you have to, give him half of my pay but he needs to work." The other guys were already in the car, ready to go but my A friend of mine was adamant about not going if I didn't go. I was standing there, not knowing what was going to happen but I knew that if anybody gave in, it would be the foreman. A friend of mine loved a good challenge and he was always defying the odds when it came to winning. This day would be no different. After ten minutes of exchanging, "He needs to work" and "Yeah, but I don't need him," the foreman finally said, "Okay, I'll find something for him to do." We both got into the car and not another word was ever spoken again regarding the matter.

When we arrived at the construction site, the foreman told me to come with him and we left. I thought he was taking me to another work site but all we did was ride from one store to another and when we were not riding, we were visiting other construction sites. When I referred to him as foreman, he made it clear to me that he was the contractor and that my buddy was actually the foreman. Now it all made sense to me. Without my buddy being at the construction site, the contractor would be stuck there giving instructions, which he couldn't afford to do. I was treated really well that day, in spite of this guy firing me a week earlier...and being forced to rehire me. He asked where I wanted to have lunch and after we had eaten, he paid the tab. I couldn't really enjoy the day because I didn't know what was on his mind.

The next day was a repeat of the day before. I didn't know whether or not the contractor was trying to get back at A friend of mine or trying to ruin our friendship by not allowing me work and paying me anyhow. I only knew that I was lifting nothing heavier than a CB radio microphone (talking with truckers), and my clothes were as clean at the end of the day as at the start. I don't think the contractor's motive really mattered to A friend of mine, so long as I was getting paid. After the third day of riding around and doing no manual labor, he asked me if I was going to be paid at the end of the week. I told him I assumed that I would but he became frustrated because I wasn't sure. He then suggested, in a not so pleasant manner, that I ask the contractor if I was going to be paid for the week. I then became frustrated with him because not knowing what the answer might be...I was afraid to ask.

I never asked about the pay but on Friday, I was handed a $350 check. I was amazed, as was A friend of mine, who asked the contractor why I he had not used me at the construction site. The contractor replied, "I told you I didn't need him." Whether he needed me or was just getting back at my buddy, I didn't know and it didn't matter. The only thing that mattered to me was I had gotten paid and I was as happy as a lark. However, the happiness would be short-lived. I spent the weekend partying like there was no tomorrow and so did the other guys in the house. No one was concerned about saving any money. It was their custom to pay the weekly rent (which I still was not paying) and then waste the remainder of their paycheck partying. If anyone needed money to get him through the following week, he simply asked the contractor for an advance in pay. This was a well-oiled machine that worked flawlessly until, unbeknownst to us, it broke down over the weekend.

10

HUNGER

When Monday morning arrived, we were all ready for work but the contractor was nowhere to be found. Phone calls to his residence yielded not so much as an answering machine. We all thought that maybe he had drunk too much over the weekend and was experiencing a serious hangover. However, when we didn't hear from him the next day, we knew something had happened...and that it wasn't good. When the failed to show up the third day, A friend of mine went to the hotel where he'd been staying but he was not there. We didn't have a clue as to why he had suddenly disappeared, leaving us without work and most important...without money.   This was on Wednesday and between the three of us (the fourth guy was from Haiti), we had less than $50 and the rent was due on Friday. The Landlord, whom I had not met, charged $50 per person each week to stay at the house. I was freeloading but that was about to end. On Friday, the guys went to the landlord and explained what had happen and she seemed very empathetic. But she made it clear that they (actually, we) could not remain at the residence rent-free and I thought she was being cruel. After all, it was no fault of ours that we had been abandoned. I was from another world but would learn later in life that sympathy does not the pay bills.

The world I was accustomed to, it was not uncommon for the neighbors to invite you into their home and give you a hot meal. And if you wanted to earn a few honest dollars, you could always rely on the local farmers to give you work. Moreover, the local hunters took delight in giving away fresh deer meat, after removing the back strap and/or antlers; or maybe even last year's kill from the freezer to make room for more. If all else failed, there were always plenty squirrel, rabbit and raccoon meat to be baked, fried and/or put on the grill. Nobody I knew from my world experienced hunger pangs. But I was now living in the city, where only the strong survive and the weak perish.

The house was quiet that weekend, as uncertainty overshadowed the desire to party. The other guys knew women in the area but I had not been there long enough to make any real acquaintances. I was mostly home alone that weekend, searching the house for things to steal and sell. I searched the guys' room thoroughly, looking for their personal items, as I was reminded of the pranks that had pulled on me at the work site. They had forgotten... but I had not. I spent most of the money I had left on food that Sunday but had already decided that I would sell the house radio the following day. The guys had nothing worth stealing, not even a watch. Maybe this accounted for why the house was never locked, which provided a perfect alibi for me, if ever accused of stealing the radio. On Monday, I stole the radio and took a bus downtown to the nearest pawn shop where I sold it for $6. I bought a $3 ham sandwich and a dollar drink from a nearby deli. As I stood on the corner eating and drinking, I contemplated returning to Willacoochee but quickly realized that I had burned all my bridges there. So, I took the bus back to College Park to ponder my next move.

The following day I spent the remainder of my (radio) money on snacks but was still hungry when I laid down that night. On Wednesday night, after having nothing to eat the entire day, A friend of mine and I went to his girlfriend's house and she cooked pork chops and made us each a sandwich. But before we left her house they got into an argument over something really trivia and he insisted that we leave…with sandwiches in hand. As we were walking back to the house, A friend of mine suddenly threw his sandwich on the ground, saying he didn't need nothing from her. I thought to myself, "Man, we starving and you throwing food away because of your pride?" Of course, I couldn't say that to him but I kept looking back…even after the sandwich had faded into the darkness. During the next two days, I wished I'd picked up that sandwich, brushed off the dirt, and eaten it.

On Thursday I ate nothing at all and couldn't find so much as a penny to buy a cookie. That night I laid down experiencing hunger pangs for the first time in my life. It was the first time I had gone 24 hours without eating. To make matters worse, the landlord came by the house early the next morning and discovered me curled in a fetal position on the couch. She asked who I was and what I was doing there. When I informed her that I was living there, she told me I had to pay $25 a week to stay, or else I was going to have to move out. Realizing the contractor had abandoned the crew and me, she did not give me a deadline; nor did she mention me paying rent for the time I'd already stayed there. In addition to being hungry, I was now facing the possibility of becoming a member of the city's homeless society. I couldn't believe this was happening to me. When the landlord left, I went to a convenient store without money but I took with me a burning desire to leave with something to eat. It was the first time I'd ever shoplifted but I walked out with a Little Debbie snack tucked under my shirt. It was the biggest gamble I had taken since playing billiards with a stranger two weeks earlier and accumulating a $125 debt with only $50 in my pocket. However, I kept playing and winning until I owed only $17.

I went back to the residence, having eaten my snack along the way, and pondered my next move. I went into the kitchen and opened the refrigerator and it was bare except for a pot with a small amount of two-week old rice in it. On the kitchen table was a bread bag with two slices of moldy bread inside. I thought about eating the rice and the bread but then thought, "I'm not going to eat this garbage." Then day turned into night and I still had not eaten anything, other than the Little Debbie snack I'd stolen from the store that morning. I thought about returning to steal something else to eat but I knew people shoplift all the time and that store clerks were fully aware of this. I decided I would look for another option but there was none other…except one.

Sometime around midnight, my stomach started aching to the point where I could no longer think about anything else other than food. I had grown accustom to the growling stomach after two days but the hunger pangs I could no longer ignore. I had to have something to eat, even if it meant risking being arrested for shoplifting. At least in jail I would be fed...but then I was concerned about other things that could happen while locked up. Then suddenly a light bulb went off in my head! Realizing it was time to drop the pride and survive, I got up and went into the kitchen and removed the pot with the rice from the refrigerator. I then added a little water, seasoned it with salt and pepper and heated it up on the stove. While it was warming, I took the slices of bread and carefully removed the molded part (wanted to preserve as much of the good stuff as possible) and then put both pieces in the oven to toast. Ten minutes later I was saying Grace and eating.

To everyone's surprise, the long-lost contractor showed up around noon the next day bearing a smile...but we didn't see anything funny. I'm sure we all wanted to pull him out of the car and have a stump party but we didn't. Seeing we were not smiling, he apologized for abandoning us and then immediately reached for his wallet...then we all smiled. He explained that his wife had left him and returned to New York and that he had taken the first available flight to be with her. Of course, no one cared about his problems. All we wanted was money so we could eat and pay the rent (I just wanted to eat). He gave me $25 and I immediately headed for the nearby Burger King. I will never forget walking inside and saying to the cashier, "I want a big hamburger and a hot apple pie." I had never been so serious in my life. I had money to buy a drink but I wasn't going to take a chance on ever being hungry again. I could get water in the city but when it came to food...it was a totally different story. If you don't work...you don't eat. For Real!

11

SOUTH FLORIDA

It was now getting cool in the city and the construction project was coming to an end. I knew I could not survive working outside during the winter months in Atlanta, nor did I consider bringing my girlfriend there. She was out of school but only 17 years old and therefore, considered a minor…although she really wanted to leave home. I had promised that I would take her away and that's what I intended to do. I knew I could be charge with Statutory Rape within the state of Georgia and kidnapping if I took her across state lines but I wasn't really concerned about any of that. As usual, I had resigned to crossing those bridges when I go to them. I just didn't want to live in Atlanta. I wanted my girlfriend and I to go someplace farther but no too far; and I wanted to be someplace where we would be virtually unknown. I decided that West Palm Beach, Florida would be the ideal place for us to live. After all, my biological father was living there for many years. I had visited him occasionally but did not have a very good relationship with him; therefore, I had not never considered living there. But now I was in need of a place of refuge and South Florida became more appealing by the day. I wrote my girlfriend from Atlanta and told her about my plan for us to be together in South Florida and she agreed.

When the construction project in Atlanta was finished, I took a bus to Douglas, Ga., where I was picked up by friends and taken to Willacoochee. I moved back in with my parents after informing them that I would leaving for West palm beach in a few days. During that time, other relatives from West Palm Beach were visiting in Douglas and had agreed to take me back with them. I checked with my girlfriend one last time to see if she was sure about leaving her five younger siblings and joining me to South Florida. She assured me that she was and the plan was put into motion. I informed my father that I would be coming to Florida but not to live with him. I would be living with the relatives who were bring me...at least for a while.

It was Sunday evening when I left for South Florida but the people with whom I was riding didn't have a clue as to what my intentions were. I was getting a free ride and would be living in a middle-class community until I could find a job and move out on my own. By now, I had accepted the fact that I have to work for living. It was only a matter of what type of work I would be doing. I helped drive the 400 plus mile trip to South Florida, although I did not have a valid driver's license. My father was thrilled that I was coming to stay (I never mentioned my girlfriend). I think he viewed my coming as a chance to reconcile but I was not the least bit interested a reconciliation. I was only interested in having a place for my girl and I to live.

The day after arriving in W.P.B., I put in an application at Burdines Dept. Store and was hired a few days later. My relative purchased the white shirt and black pants required for me to work (as a busboy) in the diner section of the store. At first, I thought I had hit the jackpot because not only was I receiving an hourly wage but the tips left on the tables as well. The people dining at these tables were not your typical fifty-cent tippers. They often tipped $1 to $3, which was very good in 1972. However, I was really embarrassed when the waitresses got together and informed me that the tips belonged to them, and that I was only to clear the tables. I thought this was wrong, since I was the one cleaning up behind these people. Nevertheless, I apologized to the waitresses but immediately devised a plan to get a portion of the tips anyway. As soon as the customer finished eating, leave a tip and walk out, I would rush over and clear the table. But while doing so, I would place a dish over the tip and scoop it up. If it were only a dollar, I would leave it but if it were $2 or more, I would take at least one dollar. I'm sure the waitresses were suspicious but I carried on as if nothing was happening and they never confronted me.

After being on the job approximately three weeks, it was time for a change. So, I quit. I told my relative that I had been laid off but I didn't tell my employer anything. To avoid a lot of questions, I moved in with my father. He was staying in one less desirable sections of West Palm Beach but it time for part two of my plan. There was a young lady living with my father and his (common law) wife at the time and we quickly became friends. I didn't tell her about my girlfriend back in Georgia, or my plans to have her meet me in Miami. My father was trying to get me hired at the landscaping company that he'd worked at since moving to Florida in the early 60's but I had other plans.

In the meantime, my new friend and I were busy touring the city during the day and playing at night. It was with her that I saw the movie, "Super Fly" for the first time. She started liking me in a manner that I knew would be only temporary because I was only interested in my girlfriend when it came to settling down.

Two weeks after moving in with my father, it was time to get my paycheck from Burdines and prepare for the next phase of my secret plan, which was to have my girlfriend join me. I couldn't just walk in and ask for my check after not calling in and giving some explanation as to why I had not reported for work for the past two week. So, I decided to tell them (employer) that I had been in an auto accident and to make it all plausible, I put small pebbles in my right shoe to create a limp. The employer expressed sympathy but of course, I had been terminated after the third day of not calling in. As soon as I left the store and was around the corner, I removed the pebbles from my shoe and headed to the bank to cash my check. After cashing it, I mailed my girlfriend money to purchase a one-way bus ticket to Miami. One week later, I boarded a southbound Greyhound bus out of West Palm Beach while my father was at work. My girlfriend was to meet me there the following day. Before I left my father's house, I stole his Saturday Night Special (cheap .22 caliber revolver). I took it for protection. I had never been to Miami and therefore, had no idea what to expect.

Upon my arrival in Miami, I walked to the Imperial Hotel, which was located in a rundown section of the city. It was near the bus depot and it was cheap. I checked in for one week, using the aliases, "Mr. & Mrs. Smith." The hotel had several floors but only one bathroom per floor. The walls of the room were not insulated, as conversation (and other doings) could be easily heard. Nevertheless, I was not ashamed and I wasn't afraid. I simply became part of the environment. My girlfriend was scheduled to arrive at the bus depot around 3:00 p.m. so I made sure I was there on time. After sitting in the lobby for approximately two hours and not seeing her, I decided to walk outside where the buses pulled into the terminal and she was standing there waiting for me. She appeared alone, frightened and lost. It was a very emotional moment for me because it was at that moments that I realized not only had she been frighten for two hours, not knowing what to expect, but had also taken a giant leap into adulthood by trusting me enough to leave home. I fought back tears, as I wondered whether or not we had made the right decision. But it was too late to turn back now.

The streets of Miami were mean and nasty. The people in the area of the city we had chosen to play husband and wife were not friendly. It was obvious that they were in survival mode in every way of life. After paying the hotel room rent for one week, I had enough money left to buy food. We even went to the theatre but had to leave early because she had a toothache. We walked the streets as though we were belonged there. I had the pistol on me at all times and therefore, was not afraid to look the people whom we passed on the street in the eye. I did so, not to see what was in their eyes but for them to see what was in mine. The message I wanted to convey was, "Don't mess with me" and I think it went over well. But to remain in Miami, I needed a job because I knew from the Atlanta experience that there very little very little love and sympathy in the city.

I worked two days at a day labor agency but I was paid only minimum wage, which was not enough to sustain my girlfriend and I. Besides that, the employment was uncertain. It all depended on who needed laborers for the day. I knew this part of my plan was not going to work so after staying in Miami one week, I devised another plan. I called my father and told him that my girlfriend and I needed to come back to West Palm Beach and live with him for a while. He was glad to know that I was coming back.

The next day we checked out of the Imperial Hotel, purchased bus tickets and headed to West Palm Beach. During the ride, very few words were exchanged between my girlfriend and I. She was probably thinking about the five siblings she'd left behind because she was the only mother they knew. I was consumed with uncertainty, as I wondered if I was ready to settle down with one person. I knew I wasn't ready to give up my freedom as a single guy but I also wanted my girlfriend. I decided that I would have both, my freedom and my girl but I couldn't have two girls living in the same house with me. I knew that upon my return, I would have to face the young lady living there, whom I'd befriended. So, I had to figure out a way to remain friends with the young lady without revealing to my girlfriend that we had dated before meeting her in Miami.

My father was all smiles, as he greeted us at the bus station. He seemed glad to have us be a part of his household but as expected, the young lady whom I'd befriended wasn't so happy. She was cold and unfriendly towards my girlfriend but she never made a scene and I never gave her a reason as to why I had not told her about my plans to unite with my girlfriend. Although she was street wise and somewhat thuggish, I think maybe it was my eyes that warned her to keep her mouth shut and treat my girlfriend with respect. I could tell she was deeply hurt by my actions but we never talked about it.

My father helped me get hired at the landscaping company where he worked from 8:00 a.m. to 4:30 p.m. Approximately, one month after we moved in with him, he rented a more spacious house in W.P. B. on Sapodilla Avenue. It was actually a rooming house with three rooms, hallway, kitchen and one bathroom. My father and his wife shared one room, my girlfriend and I another, and the young lady the other. I never had anything to do with the young lady while we were all living under the same roof...but she did imply (to my girl) that she and I had been romantically involved, which I denied. When I confronted her, she denied that she had said anything to my girlfriend and it never happened again. After three months, she moved out and went to live with her older sister.

12

66 FORD FAIRLANE

My brother, Nate, came to South Florida one year later and got a job building mattresses at Palm Beach Bedding. Not long after, I quit the landscaping job and was hired by the same company to build box springs mattresses. I really liked the job because it was challenging. I was paid a basic hourly rate plus production. Each (unassembled) box spring had a label attached with a number indicating how many minutes it should take to build the unit. Each label was removed, glued to a form and tallied at the end of the day. Any minutes exceeding 480 were considered production. I was fast and would often build the unit in half the allotted time…but some units did not have labels attached and I used this to my advantage. I would make up bogus labels and attach them to my sheet and no one ever questioned me. Although I was cheating the company, I was dutiful and seldom missed work. For the first time in my life, I looked forward to going to work.

I even got a part-time job at a large retail store, working as a catalogue clerk during that time, which I also enjoyed. Customers who order from the catalogue would come to the store to get their packages. My duty included retrieving their package from the back and collecting their money (cash and checks). At first I was honest but then I started wanting things I could not afford, so I devised a plan to take a part of the cash I was collecting.

My father had given me a 1965 Chevrolet Corvair but the left rear tire leaned at an angled that suggested it might (literally) break at any moment. However, the engine ran smooth and the driving wasn't that bad…but it was just the thought that whatever the tire was attached to might give way in the middle of traffic. Other than an occasional drive around the block to keep the battery from dying, I wanted nothing to do with this contraption. My father owned an olive green 1966 Ford Fairlane 289 V8 coupe at the time but by his own admission, he never kept a car too long. When he decided to ditch the Ford Fairlane for something else, he offered to sell it to me for $200 and I accepted. It was a good car but I hated the color. Within 6 months, this ordinary Ford Fairlane had been transformed into one very "Mean Street Machine." Its makeover included chrome/mag wheels, new tires (wide rears), a 1968 Barracuda Blue paint job, yellow traction bars, engine high rise intake manifold, electric fuel pump, dual distributor, four-barrel carburetor, headers, Thrust pipes, chrome manifold covers, ¾ cam, new seat covers, and new carpet. Nate did all the mechanical work, with the exception of installing the ¾ cam…and the retail store was the unwilling sponsor.

Although I was working part-time at the department store, there were times when I brought home more money than I earned at the bedding company. The difference being, I did not earn half the money I brought home from retailer…I stole it. I would sometimes take as much as $200 a week from the cash register while in full view of the senior clerk. Twenty-dollar bills were kept in the same section of the register as the checks but instead of separating them before the count, I would grab everything and go into a back room and quickly removed several $20 bills before returning to the front to rejoin the clerk. If I was working alone, I never took a dime…for obvious reasons. It was not uncommon for me to spend $200 to $300 a week on car parts. This lasted for several months before management took preventative measures. But by then I had added everything to my car that I could think of, including a floor mounted 8-track player…and lots of fanfare. Although the car was modified for speed, I never raced anyone. I just wanted to show it off and be the envy of the town. The crippled Corvair, I eventually sold for $50 to a co-worker at the bedding company whom we called "Ham Bone."

13

GETTING HIGH

One of the things I really liked about South Florida was the marijuana. A $5 (nickel) bag, equivalent to 2.5 grams, yielded at least five joints. An ounce cost between $30 to $40, depending on the grade/potency, and lasted at least a week. I only smoked marijuana occasionally before I left home but I will never forget my first high. Me, along with three other guys rode into the wood off Springhead Road in my car and smoked a joint. I remember feeling as though I was floating in slow motion as I drove back to the main highway. The high was good and lasted approximately 4 hours but when I was coming down, I noticed a serious change in my attitude. I think maybe it was an attempt to conquer my fear of being on my own that led to my dependence on marijuana once I relocated to South Florida.

I learned early how to distinguish the good stuff for the bad (babbit) by using both sight and smell but the real test was in the smoking. On rare occasions, I would score a bad nickel bag but the ounces I made sure was high grade. Sometimes, good weed made me laugh at things that were ordinarily not funny but mostly it just meddled me out, taking me to another world...where everything was well defined and crystal clear. It enhanced the sound of the music I loved and it steadied my hand, as I transferred images from my mind onto paper; and my thoughts into poetry and lyrics. The following poem I wrote in 1974 while high on marijana:

THE GHETTO

This life in the ghetto is surely hell on earth,
There's no mercy for man, woman, boy or girl.
In these jaws of death there is no escape,
Men being killed and women getting raped.

Men working hard on some jive A** job,
Only to get paid and then get robbed.
Women have to work just to make ends meet,
But still borrow cups of rice until next week.

The girls leave home at the age of twelve,
To be seduced by a pimp and forced to sell.
The boys join gangs, trying to rule the streets,
They end up in prison or covered with sheets.

Pushers say their dope is the best in town,
Giving free hits to get you chained and bound.
Junkies stealing from their mama to buy cocaine,
Smoking all daddy's weed but it's not the same.

There's also Reverend Jones who drives a big Cadillac,
He lives in brick mansion but it's across the tracks.
He can heal the sick with the touch of his hand,
But can't lead us out the ghetto to the Promise Land.

Sometimes I wrote in journals, recording my perception of people, places and thing. But after being taken so high, I often descended back down to earth and into a state of both fear and depression. Being a young man in the city with no education or work experience was frightening. Although my girlfriend and I lived with my father, and he seemed very pleased to have us there, I wanted more than what I saw in him. But how to get more out of life, I had not a clue. I feared becoming like my father, whose life was little more than working, coming home at the end of the day, having a couple of beers, bathing, eating, watching TV and going to bed between 9:00 p.m. and 10:00 p.m. The next day, he would do it all over again. I was often depressed because I saw no way to avoid becoming like him.

Although I drank beer and would occasionally get drunk, I was not a lover of alcoholic beverages. I hated the taste of alcohol and I didn't like the way it made me feel but sometimes I would drink more than I could handle…depending on what was happening with me and my girlfriend. Sometimes, while hanging out with other people, I would over indulge but usually waited until I got home to vomit. Beer was my drink of choice but I never drunk more than four 12 ounce bottles (or cans) unless I was depressed, angry, or just seeking sympathy. I experimented with THC (a horse tranquilizer in pill form) a few times before realizing one day while playing pool on Rosemary Avenue (the meanest street in WPB at the time), that it wasn't for me. My brother and I were playing pool when suddenly I didn't know what to do with the cue stick in my hand; nor did I know why I was at the pool hall. Fortunately for me, my brother was able to get us both back home. It was the last time I took THC. Black Beauties (speed) gave me a sense of well-being but the effects lasted too long, as they kept me awake when I wanted to sleep. Vodka was practically tasteless when mixed well with orange juice but the adverse effect of not tasting the alcohol was I would drink too much and therefore, have a serious hangover the next day. There was no such side effect when I smoked marijuana.

Although I lived to get high, during my early years in South Florida, I was always sober on the job. I would always wait until I was home (or on my way) to smoke marijuana so I could enjoy the high while I relaxed. There was no drug testing in those days, so one could get as high as a kite...so long as one's behavior did not reveal anything out of the ordinary. When I came down off the high, I was often mean and hard to get along with. I would pick arguments with my girlfriend over trivia things...such as old boyfriends, or food not being prepared to my liking. When I came in from work, I would often be angry and I didn't know why. One day, I prayed and asked God to help me be kinder to my girlfriend...and He did. I eventually stopped being angry (without reason) when I came in from work. My girlfriend wasn't working at the time but that was not the problem, nor did I want her to. I was just mean! When a guy refused to pay me a $1 bet when I won a pool game, I broke the pool stick over his head and ran. I struck him not because I needed (or even wanted) the money. It was the principle of it. I fled the scene when he reached into his pocket; otherwise, I would have grabbed another cue stick and hit him again.

14

IN A CERTAIN CITY

Approximately two years after moving to Palm Beach County, my brother and I learned that we had cousins from Georgia who were staying in a certain City, Fl. He and I would often visit them on weekends, leaving on Friday evening (after work) and return late Sunday evening. A certain City was known as the "Hood" with all the trimmings. It was a crime-ridden, drug infested, poverty-stricken section of Miami but I was never afraid when we were there. My brother and I would often meet young ladies and date them over the weekend without fear of encountering jealous boyfriends. I always carried a concealed .25 automatic handgun with the hope that if attacked, I would "take out" at least one assailant before being taken out.

A friend of mine had left Atlanta and was now also living in the Miami area. He'd left soon after I moved to South Florida and as usual, he still no problem fighting anybody who challenged him...or someone whom he just didn't like. It was not uncommon for him, while riding through A certain City with my brother and I, to stick his head out the window and make passes at females walking with male companions. If the guy said something, not only would A friend of mine hurl profanities at him, he would demand we stop the car and let him out, which we would. After a brief exchange of words, a physical altercation would ensue, while my brother and I sat in the car pleading, "Man, Let's Go!" We were totally strangers in the neighborhood and I expected any moment for friends of the other guy to come running with guns in hand, blazing away. During the fight, bottles would be broken and the two combatants would be rolling on concrete and shards of glass as if they were rolling on the grass. After five or so minutes of trying to kill each other, the fight would end as suddenly as it began and everybody would be on their way...as if the battle was only a test of manhood.

A friend of mine had a wife and child in Miami and he worked in construction but he was a street person, meaning he was street wise. He could often sense when something was about to go down before it actually happened. He and I were playing pool one day in Miami when suddenly he dropped the cue stick and whispered to me in a demanding tone, "Let's Go! They fixing to raid this place." Two minutes later, while hastily walking away, we saw law enforcement surrounding the place. A friend of mine was also a hustler. On another occasion when we were playing pool, a guy walked up and placed a $5 bet on me. A friend of mine gave me a signal, indicating I should lose so he could win the bet and I did. When the guy discovered he had been duped, he refused to pay and it led to a serious physical altercation, which resulted in the police being called. We both fled the scene...but that was the last time I hung out with him in Miami. Shortly after that incident, my cousins moved from A certain City, which probably saved my life. Although A friend of mine was brave and fearless, the mean streets of Miami would prove to be too much for even him. Just as he'd rescued me from being beat up by the ex-Marine in Atlanta, and had gotten me rehired after being fired...I would return the favor by helping him escape Miami... with his life.

It was around 11:00 p.m. when A friend of mine knocked on the door of my father's home in WPB, after everyone had gone to bed. He had been stabbed in the neck with a butcher knife a week earlier while fighting in the streets of Miami and was now on the run. He needed my brother and I to take him back to Miami to get his wife and infant son. He told us the guy that stabbed him, along with his friends, were now looking for him so they could finish him off. I had never seen him so vulnerable in all the years I'd known him. He had a serious wound, the knife having missed his aorta by a mere two centimeters. Because he had come to my aid, not once but twice, in Atlanta, it was the perfect opportunity to show my gratitude. My brother and I, along with our girlfriends, headed south on I-95 with him in the car to rescue his family around midnight. I brought along a 16-shot .22 semi-automatic rifle and a cheap 6-shot .25 semi-automation handgun...just in case things got ugly. These meager weapons were all we had but they were better than a butcher knife and definitely better than no weapon at all. Barely a word was spoken during the 60-mile trip to Miami but I remember thinking it could very well be my last ride. We had brought along our girlfriends because although A friend of mine and his family lived in the same neighborhood as his assailant, no threats had been made against his family; therefore, we felt it would be safe for the ladies to help his wife get the few things we could bring back in the car.

The plan was for us to send the ladies up to the apartment while we sat in the car and watched. When asked if they were afraid and they both assured us that they were not. When we arrived at the designated spot, we watched as the they made their way upstairs to the dark apartment. A few minutes after entering, they started bringing clothes out to the car. After making four or five trips to and from the apartment, A friend of mine's wife and baby accompanied our girlfriends to the car. During the long and mostly quiet ride back to WPB, it was decided that my brother would take A friend of mine's wife and child to Belle Glade, Fl. (where her father lived) the next day and we would take him to Willacoochee.

He told us during the eight-hour drive to Willacoochee how the guy had gotten him on the ground and stabbed him in the neck. He also talked about how helpless he was and knew he was about to die…when a miracle happened. Before the angry young man could stab him again, someone from the crowd took the knife away, thus saving his life. To my amazement, he accredited God for saving his life and he vowed that day to change his ways. I'm not sure as to whether or not he changed his ways…but I do know he never lived in Miami again.

15

FATHERHOOD

During the summer of 1974, my girlfriend stated complaining about stomach pains and wanted to go to the emergency room. Thinking she was just experiencing female problems, I reluctantly took her to the hospital to be examined. She was not one to complain about anything so in the back of my mind, I was hoping nothing serious was going on. When she was called into the examination room, I remained in the waiting room. I was thinking about what I was going to do when we left. An hour later, she came back into the waiting room appearing as if everything was normal. I was sure it was a wasted trip but as I rose to leave she said, "I'm pregnant." Although we had been having sex for the past two years without any form of birth control, I was in denial. That denial quickly turned to anger because I was not ready to be a father. We had only recently gotten married and now I was going to be a father. I wasn't even ready to be a husband and had it not been for the urging of my father, we would have continued "shacking up" like him. He wasn't married to the woman he was living with for several years...but it was his house.

Settling down was the last thing on my mind when I convinced my girlfriend to abandon her family in Georgia and join me in Florida. I had claimed her as my own and I wanted her there with me but mainly to stay at home while I roam the streets of Palm Beach County, doing any and everything I was old enough and wanted to do. We had gotten married because my father, under pressure from my mother, said we had to marry or find another place to stay. So, marry we did. The ceremony was performed at the presiding minister's home and I gave absolutely no thought to the vows I recited. There were no rings to exchange and there was no honeymoon. I never considered, or asked my wife how she felt about anything. It was all about me. After the wedding ceremony, we went to a drive-in movie. I did so in defiance of having to get married. It was my way of saying I had no regard for the vows I'd just exchanged. But I think she was happy that we were husband and wife, regardless of the circumstances.

After a few days of learning I would be a father, the anger started to subside and I gradually became a very proud expectant father-to-be. I thought about the life I'd created, as I anxiously awaited its arrival. I hoped it would be a boy and deep down in my soul, I felt that it was. In fact, I was so sure that I chose a name in advance, which came to me in a dream…but I was still not ready for fatherhood. I was just not ready for the responsibility. I was married but I still wanted to be single. I didn't want to be "tied down" or committed to just one woman but I demanded commitment from my wife. I wanted to put her on a shelf while I "played" the field and that's exactly what I did. One night, I didn't come home until the next morning and when I saw her lying in bed, 8 months pregnant, I was saddened. She was clearly holding back tears and I made a silent vow to never stay out all night again…but it was a vow that I would not keep.

It was during the early morning of March 10, 1975 that I took my wife to St. Mary's Hospital to give birth. I dropped her off and came back home to wait until she had the baby. As I mentioned previously, I was very selfish and thought it a waste of time to sit around in the hospital's waiting room. I preferred to be back home doing something else, if only sleeping. At some point during the day, I called the hospital and was told my wife had given birth to a baby boy. I was overflowing with joy, as I rushed to see what the baby looked like. I wanted to see the life I had created. As for my wife, I assumed she was fine because I felt like giving birth was something women were created to do; therefore, I was not really concerned about her…but not in a mean way. I just thought women handled their business and men handled theirs. When I arrived at the hospital, I went directly to the nursery and saw a baby boy with a tag or label that had "Williams" attached to the crib. I admired the newborn but did not feel a connection. I really wasn't very happy with what I saw but I knew I had to live with it. I tried to make myself happy but I felt no joy at all. My gut told me that something was just not right.

I left the nursery and went to see my wife, who appeared to have been traumatized. I asked how she was doing and she said she was doing okay. She had a smile on her face, so I knew she was happy, either because she was a mother, or that ordeal was over. I told her I had seen the baby and that he had long legs. That's about all I said before leaving for the day. As I drove back home and for the remainder of the day, I wondered why I had this strange feeling about the baby I saw in the nursery. When I visited my wife the next day, she was breast feeding the baby and smiling. As I drew closer to get a look at the baby, I realized it was not the same baby I'd seen in the nursery the day before. I immediately felt a strong bond with this child and was now welled pleased. I named the baby boy, Caraus Cornell Williams. He was very cute and I was proud to call him my son. My wife and I had shared a twin bed since moving in with my father on Sapodilla Ave. but now it was time to make a move. The small room we lived in had no space for a crib and three people sleeping on the twin bed was all but impossible; therefore, I had no other option but to move out on my own.

16

IRRESPONSIBILITY

Not long after our son was born, we moved into our first apartment, which was approximately 2 miles away from my Dad's house. It was a small, wooden, one-bedroom apartment adjacent to another apartment separated by uninsulated walls. The landlady was a 75-year old wise woman that took a liking to us immediately...probably because of the baby. Needless to say, I would use her kindness to my benefit, as I was often late paying the rent. But I loved hosting marijuana parties, having several people gathered at the apartment, getting high while listening to loud music and staring at a disco probe light. My wife and son were usually in the bedroom because she didn't smoke marijuana. Life for me was one big party, which meant I had all my priorities in the wrong place. I loved getting high and listening to music, and drawing, and assembling and painting plastic models.

It was always pleasure before business with me. I made enough money to pay the rent and utilities but I was selfish and very irresponsible. I bought nice things for the apartment to satisfy my taste, as well as to impress others. When high on marijuana, I could feel the music and I often related to most of the lyrics. I had no problem drawing any image that formed in my mind and when I assembled plastic models, I gave them life when I was high. I gave my son very little attention, except when taking his picture. I gave him virtually no consideration, as I would often blast music loud enough for the neighbors to hear. I was busy doing what I wanted to do, while his mother nurtured him…giving him the necessary love and tender care every child need and deserves.

When I couldn't get my way, I was often very mean and destructive. On one occasion, my father's common law wife wanted to come and visit us but I wanted to work on assembling and painting a scale model ship. When my wife told me that she wanted them to come over, I went into a rage and punched a mirror twice, severely cutting the fingers on my right hand. When they arrived, I was sitting on the bed, bleeding and crying inconsolably. They wanted me to go to the hospital but I refused. I knew if I sought medical attention, and told them what I had done, I would be referred to the mental facility a.k.a. 45th Street. I f refused to tell them what happened, the hospital staff would notify the police and I could let that happen for two reasons. One, I didn't need a "crazy" file on me and two, I was to start work the next day full time at Sears. My hands were bandaged and when I reported for work the next day, I told my employer that I had fallen off a skate board onto glass and cut my hand. The next time I went into a rage, my wife simply called my name, touched me and sat me on the bed…and I calmed down.

The 66 Ford Fairland was equipped for racing but I never raced anyone. It was used strictly for transportation and therefore, would occasionally break down while going to and from work. One day, I left work on a lunch break and on the way back it shut off in the middle of a busy avenue and wouldn't start. It just happened that it stopped in front of a used car lot. I walked over to the dealership and after the mechanic help get my car onto the lot, I offered to trade it on the spot. The salesman raised the hood and immediately agreed to accept it as a trade-in with no money down. On the lot was a white 1971 Mercury Capri that had to be jumpstarted and without doing a test drive, I signed all the necessary papers and drove away. Two weeks later, I returned the car to the dealership because it was "skipping" really bad and I demanded they give back my car (66 Ford) …but it had been sold already. I was in a rage, yelling that I was not driving the Capri off the lot because I didn't want it anymore. A mechanic came out, lifted the hood and discovered a disconnected spark plug wire. After reconnecting the wire, the car purred like a kitten and I drove away smiling; however, the smile would not last. A month later, the transmission went out and I was furious but this time, I did not return to the dealership. I just refused to pay for the car, which led to it being repossessed. Fortunately for me, my father loaned me the used van he'd purchased from the local Southern Bell company.

Although I was working part-time department store and cleaning offices at night, I was very irresponsible when it came to paying bills. I did not see the importance of paying rent on time. I could tell that my landlady was getting frustrated with me when she had to ask for the rent…and when I allowed the water to be shut off. The light bill was included in the rent.

Because I was irresponsible, I never kept a job very long. Besides being irresponsible, I just didn't like anyone telling me what to do. I had several jobs where I simply walked off or forced the employer to fire me. I was hired as an on-the-job auto body repairman prior to moving my family into the one-room apartment. But due to my refusal to report for work, I was fired after only 3 months. My supervisor liked me and tried to help me but eventually said to me, "You just won't come to work." Afterwards, I was hired fulltime to pump gas at the local mall but I hated wearing uniforms; therefore, I was constantly calling in saying I couldn't come to work for one reason or another. When I did go in, I found a way to steal some of the money I collected at the gas pumps. Of course, stealing from my employer was nothing new for me.

17

ANGRY YOUNG BLACK MAN

I was hired full time as a shipping clerk at department store but I wanted to be a salesman, working with my mind rather than my hands and back. I reported to work every day on time in an attempt to prove that I was reliable. I expected it would take six months to convinced my employer that I was serious about "moving up" in the company. I only had a high school education but I was friends with three black men working there that were not doing manual labor. One was a college graduate and was a department manager. Actually, he's the one that hired me to work part-time in the catalogue department I was stealing money from. Another black guy working there had gone to college but I'm not sure whether or not he had earned degree. The third guy, I knew only had only a high school education but he was a salesman. I always assumed he had been given that position because Sears needed more color on the floor. He dressed nice but other than "Yes Sir" and "Yes Ma'am," he wasn't very professional. Nevertheless, I knew my time would come to shine as top notch salesman. In the meantime, I would perform my duties as a shipping clerk like none others before me.

Even when no one was watching me, I worked as though the company belonged to me. Although I had previously stolen from my employer, I was now all about business and doing the right thing. I knew I had more to offer the world than my back and I wanted a chance to prove it. I especially did not like wearing a uniform because to me it was tantamount to wearing shackles and the company's name on label, I liken to a chain. I did not like the feeling of being owned by anyone. There was another black man there working in the warehouse (in another department) who impressed me as never finishing high school and he worked like a slave, doing the job of at least two men. I was determined not to become like him. When I asked him why he allowed the company to work him so hard his reply was, "That's just the way it is." And he quickly walked away…as if he was afraid to be seen talking to me. I wanted to wear my own clothes and I wanted to be as clean at the end of my shift as in the beginning. But mostly, I wanted to exercise my ability to make a living using my mind but it was not to be, at least not at this retailer.

After serving my (self) allotted six months of hard labor, I applied for a salesman position but my requests to be promoted fell upon deaf ears. I continued doing my appointed job to the best of my ability because it was not all bad. I was not lifting constantly like the "That's the way it is" guy. Most of my duties involved doing paperwork, which really was not bad but I wanted what I wanted and that was to be moved from the warehouse and placed on the floor as a salesman. Added to my frustration was my elderly white supervisor sleeping on the job while I did the manual labor. I reported him to his superiors but to no avail.

The operation manager would let me see him watching my sleeping supervisor from overhead but nothing changed. It was during that time that I learned about the unwritten policy (what I came to believe) designed especially for a few select employees in the work place. Back home, I knew it as the "good ol' boy" system but in the city, it was just a bit more sophisticated and not quite as obvious. To compensate for doing 85 percent of the work, while the supervisor slept, I started intercepting returned gold jewelry were sent to the department for shipping...but I continued to work hard.

One day while helping a co-worker lift a rug, I felt a sharp pain in my neck that caused me to drop it. I reported the injury but did not seek medical attention at the time but after a month or so, the pain had started causing me to lose sleep at night. I called in sick on three consecutive days and without conferring with my employer, I made an appointment to see a chiropractor, who referred me to a workers' compensation attorney. When I returned to work, I was called into the office and told by the assistant general manager that my employment was being terminated. The reason given was because I had parked in the store's main parking lot, which was against company policy. I knew that but this was a rainy day but I also knew it was not uncommon for "certain" employees to violate that policy on rainy days. There was no doubt in my mind that this guy was firing me because of the reported injury. Shivering from being wet and sitting in his air-conditioned office, I made it clear to him that I was not shaking out of fear, but rather because I was cold. I also told him that I would not bow down to him. He stated that he did not want me to bow down to him and when I informed him that I had made an appointment with a chiropractor, he asked, "What good will he do you?" He then told me to move my car and report to my work area, where I was placed on light duty… but I was angry.

I was angry because I had given my all, with the hopes of being promoted and the reward I received for my effort was an attempt to get rid of me…as if I never existed. After two weeks of light duty, I was sent back to the shipping department to perform my regular duties. I filed a claim against my employer with the Urban League. A month later, I received a reply informing me that they had investigated but found nothing indicating I was being discriminated against or mistreated because of my race. That day, I became an angry young black man and would eventually be fired for insubordination, which is exactly what I wanted. I'd heard employers could not fire employees injured on the job but I was determined to change that because I wanted something for the retailer to pay for what they were doing to me. Unfortunately, I did not receive the workers' compensation benefits I'd expected and when I applied for unemployment benefits, I was denied. The reason given for the latter was I had to be physically able and willing to work in order to receive benefits. This only added fueled to my anger.

I told my landlady that I had injured my back on the job and that I was suing my former employer. I informed her so that she wouldn't pressure me for the rent, although I was still working part-time. She said to me that day, "Son, I tell ya, everything is a racket. The doctor is a racket. The lawyer is a racket and some of the churches is a racket." I felt as though she probably knew what she was talking about but I just didn't want her hassling me about the rent. Whenever the water was shut off due nonpayment, I got water to cook, bath and flush the toilet from the spigot in backyard of the apartment. When the landlord discovered this, she placed a huge German Shepard in the backyard and warned me that it would bite. I then started getting water from my neighbor living next door and when the landlady heard about it, she said we had to move. I didn't think she would evict us because of the baby and when she did, I was angry with her. She was probably angry with me as well for being such a sorry man, husband and father. Now, I was without a full-time job and was being evicted... but my wife had a job.

I moved my family across town and into a three-story wooden apartment building on Hibiscus Street. The rent was $40 a week, which included lights and water. Our apartment was located on the first floor, which both good and bad. It was good because there was no elevator in the aging building. It was bad because on hot muggy nights, we had to sleep with the windows up if we wanted the electric fan to circulate fresh air. The apartment consisted of a living room, kitchen area, bathroom and a bedroom. Having the window raised at night would later prove to be a mistake...for some women.

On Friday evening, the landlord would knock on doors, collecting the rent. He was a friendly man but he was also a business man. When he came for the rent, he did not accept excuses as payment. I knew this landlord would not buy into any of my sob stories, so I made sure the rent was paid from the money my wife earned. She worked with my father's common law wife at a nearby assisted living home for nuns. After consulting with a WC attorney, I quit my part-time job when he assured me that I had a good case against my employer. I took that to mean I would receive a huge settlement in the near future. In the meantime, I stayed at home all day assembling and painting plastic models. Other than being in place when my son home in from kindergarten, and working occasionally for the landlord in lewd of the rent, I contributed nothing the household while waiting for my big settlement. Every time I consulted with my attorney, he assured me that things were going well and that I should continue seeing the chiropractor. So, I continued to stay inside during the day, coming out at night only to play.

After waiting months to receive the settlement, I got tired of waiting and decided to get a job. The friend I'd met while working at the department store, was now working at an alcoholism rehabilitation center, located the next street over behind the apartment I was living. I was hired as a van driver on the 3:00 p.m. to 11:00 p.m. shift. My duties included transporting clients to and from AA meetings, doctor appointments, and delivering dinner to three in house treatment facilities. I was usually off on weekends.

A few months after I started working at the rehab center, a lady living in our apartment building was sexually assaulted. The assailant had entered through her window during the wee hours of the morning and held a knife to her throat while he raped her. Although the lady reported the assault to the police and was taken to the hospital to be examined, his was 1978 and DNA was unheard of. I had recently purchased a Heritage Rough Rider .22/.22 mag "cowboy pistol" revolver but had never fired it. When I heard about the assault, I took it back to the gun shop and traded it for a 5-shot .38 revolver that same day. Although I had not fired the cowboy pistol, it was considered used by the gun dealer; therefore, it was worth only 75% of what I paid for it. I was angry about getting ripped off but felt I had no other choice but to get a pistol with more stopping power.

While driving up to the apartment late one Saturday night, I was met by my wife and son running from the apartment. She was not properly dress so I knew something was wrong. She told me that she had been awoken by someone coming through the window and when she called out to my brother, who was home on leave from the Army Reserve, the intruder fled into the night. I was so angry that I fired a shot into the air, as if calling the coward out to face me. I was livid but soon calmed down after realizing I should have been there. But I became determined to find out who it was that had disrespected me by attempting to violate my wife. Since meeting her, I had always protected her from both male and female...even her father. When she told me that the guy living next door to us (at my father's house) was hitting on her while I was at work, I confronted him immediately and he apologized. My wife would later tell me that he never so much as said "Good Morning" to her afterwards. When an elderly gentleman called the house in the wee hours of the morning, threatening to tell my wife about the plans he heard his girlfriend (who was crying in the background) and I making to meet, I told him if he showed up at my daddy's place (where we were living) that I would blow his head off. He hung up and I never heard anything else about the incident. None of my many female acquaintances ever contacted my wife. I always told them that if they ever disrespected her in any way, that they would regret it. I was not about to let this creep get away with trying to come into my apartment uninvited.

After the police left that night, I noticed this one guy sitting on the steps of the apartment building and my instinct told me he was the guy. I was thinking that the assailant was likely someone living it the same building. All I had to do was wait and in time, I would know who it was. Based on nothing but a gut feeling, I declared the guy sitting on the steps that night…guilty. My wife could not identify him because it was dark but said it could've been him. I decided that if he was not the right guy, then it would fall under category of, "That's too bad" because in my mind he was the one. He lived on the third floor and when I learned what apartment he was in, I started harassing him. I told the other tenants that he was the assailant and when he heard I was accusing him, he came to me and swore he was innocent. I told him that I didn't believe him and that he should move…find another place to live. When he replied, "But I don't have anywhere to go," I knew he was guilty. I then pointed my index finger at him and lifted my thumb, signifying that I was going to shoot him and I walked away. After our encounter, several people whom he had told about our little talk, came to his defense but I was convinced that he was guilty and I made that known.

Two weeks later, he still had not moved so I took the threat to another level. I started secretly placing threatening notes on his door during the day while he was (I assume) working. The notes contained not only threatening words but violent images of mayhem as well. I took extra care as to not provide him evidence to take to the police. When the notes failed to convince him to move, I started placing small pumpkins in front of his door (one every other day) with faces drawn on them. In the eyes and ears of these drawn faces, I inserted steak knives and around the entry points, I put red paint to simulate blood. One month after the attempted assault on my wife, the guy whom I suspected moved...and I never saw or heard from him again.

In the meantime, the chiropractor referred me to a neurologist who subjected to me to an experiment that involved cortisone shots in the back. The pain was unbearable but it was too late to back out. As I twisted and moan, the physician inflicting the pain was yelling at me to stay still. When he was finished, I had to be placed in a wheel chair and helped into the van by the guy who had help me get hired at the rehab center. I didn't really mind the pain because I knew my huge settlement was just around the corner. A few weeks after receiving the shots in the back, my attorney called me to his office to discuss my case. He was friendly when I walked in but no sooner than I sat down, he started to tell me about how my "alleged" injury was superficial; therefore, my case was worth (after his fees) only $900 because I really had no case. When I told him I would not settle for that amount, he stared me in the eyes as if to say, "We both know there's nothing wrong with you." But as I'd won the staring contest with the Native American (while in the Army) I won this one too. He finally admitted that my former employer was not willing to pay any more for my injury and that I should accept the offer. Knowing I wasn't really hurt, I agree to the $900 settlement...but this was not the end of the story.

Two weeks after agreeing to the meager settlement, the attorney's secretary called and informed me that the settlement check had been sent to the chiropractor's office by mistake. She added that I should go to his office and sign it over to him. I said to her, "Tell that little fat man [attorney] that if he don't get that check to me, I'll report his slick A** to the Florida Bar Association." Sensing he was a shady character after our last meeting, I had already gathered information as to how to file a complaint against him. Immediately following the conversation with his secretary, I wrote a letter to the Florida Bar Association, complaining about how he was trying to take advantage of me because I was black. Two weeks later, the settlement check arrived in the mail. Now, I was angrier than I'd ever been, as I deemed "system" aka corporate America the enemy. I trusted absolutely no one in the corporate world, whether they were black or white. In my mind, I was still as slave. The physical shackles and chains had been removed and replaced with policies...held by men who had the power to determine whether I live or merely exist. Since leaving high school, I'd had at least twenty jobs over an eight-year period. Some had lasted two hours, some two days, some two months but I had not worked on any job full-time for more than one year.

With the exception of the eight months I was in Job Corps, I had been a very angry young black man since June 3, 1970, the day after graduating high school...but that was about to change. When my wife informed me that she was pregnant with our second child, I decided to give life another chance by trying to become a productive member of society...again.

AUTHOR BIOGRAPHY

Harvey Williams Jr. was born July 11, 1952 in Willacoochee, Ga. In 1972, he moved to South Florida in search of a better life. After losing his family in 1984, he became addicted to crack (cocaine) and homeless. With little more than the clothes on his back, he returned home in 1986 and became a born again Christian. Today, he is married and the father of four. He's also the pastor of House of Deliverance Church in Willacoochee, Ga. In 2007, he became a published author by writing, "From Pusher to Preacher (By the Grace of God) Pt. 2," followed by "Sarah (Slipping into Darkness)" in 2009, and "Views of A Southern Black Man" in 2015. Mr. Williams is also a columnist for the Atkinson County Citizen, writing weekly editorials since 2002. His hobbies include, traveling, photography and coin collecting.

Printed in the United States
By Bookmasters